CARING
IN CRISIS:

Bible Studies for Helping People

Judith Allen Shelly

InterVarsity Press
Downers Grove
Illinois 60515

InterVarsity Press is the book-publishing division of Inter-Varsity Christian Fellowship, a student movement active on campus at hundreds of universities, colleges and schools of nursing. For information about local and regional activities, write IVCF, 233 Langdon St., Madison, WI 53703.

All Scripture quotations are from the Revised Standard Version of the Bible, copyrighted 1946, 1952, © 1971, 1973 or from the Good News Bible—Old Testament: Copyright © American Bible Society 1976; New Testament: Copyright © American Bible Society 1966, 1971, 1976; Today's English Version (TEV).

Distributed in Canada through InterVarsity Press, 1875 Leslie St., Unit 10, Don Mills, Ontario M3B 2M5, Canada.

ISBN 0-87784-563-8
Library of Congress Catalog Card Number: 78-13878

Printed in the United States of America

19	18	17	16	15	14	13	12	11	10	9	8	7	6	5	4
95	94	93	92	91	90	89	88	87	86	85	84	83	82		

Week One: Responsible Caring   *11*

Day One: Our Mandate   *12*

Day Two: Our Focus   *14*

Day Three: Being a Servant   *16*

Day Four: Living in a Pluralistic World   *18*

Day Five: The Religious Instinct   *20*

Day Six: A Dying Man Prays to God   *22*

Group Discussion: Responsible Caring   *24*

Week Two: What Is Human?   *25*

Day One: Created in God's Image   *26*

Day Two: Disobedient Creatures   *28*

Day Three: Known by God   *30*

Day Four: An Integrated Whole   *32*

Day Five: Loved and Formed by God   *34*

Day Six: Redeemed by God   *36*

Group Discussion: What Is Human?   *38*

Week Three: Identifying Spiritual Needs   *39*

Day One: The Need for Meaning and Purpose   *40*

Day Two: The Source of Meaning and Purpose   *42*

Day Three: The Source of Love   *44*

Day Four: The Meaning of Love   *46*

Day Five: Our Need for Forgiveness   *48*

Day Six: The Way of Forgiveness   *50*

Group Discussion: Identifying Spiritual Needs   *52*

Week Four: Meeting Spiritual Needs **53**

Day One: Setting Priorities *54*

Day Two: A Psalmist's View of His Spiritual Needs *56*

Day Three: Assessing a Spiritual Need *58*

Day Four: Caring for the Whole Person *60*

Day Five: Thoughts of a Suffering Person *62*

Day Six: A Person in Anguish *64*

Group Discussion: Meeting Spiritual Needs *66*

Week Five: Resources for Helping People **67**

Day One: Yourself *68*

Day Two: Prayer I *70*

Day Three: Prayer II *72*

Day Four: Scripture: Its Purpose and Power *74*

Day Five: Scripture: Its Impact *76*

Day Six: Other Christians *78*

Group Discussion: Resources for Helping People *80*

Week Six: Personal Resources **81**

Day One: Past Experiences *82*

Day Two: A God-given Ministry *84*

Day Three: God's Spirit in You *86*

Day Four: Participants in God's Purpose and Plan *88*

Day Five: God's Armor *90*

Day Six: The Lord, Our Shepherd *92*

Group Discussion: Personal Resources *94*

Introduction

Crisis.
A friend is in a car accident.
Crisis.
Your father loses his job.
Crisis.
Your pastor announces he and his wife are getting a divorce.

We all meet crises directly or indirectly. Someone close to us faces a situation starkly outside their normal patterns and expectations of life. At such times of stress, emotional, physical and spiritual equilibrium begin shaking. Tempers get shorter. Headaches become more frequent. Prayer sometimes disappears.

Often we want to help. We care for the people involved. But we don't know what to do. We don't know how to offer support. What resources can we draw on? How can we apply the proper remedy to a given problem?

Even people who are not normally concerned with religious

matters suddenly begin asking questions about God or blaming God in times of stress. How can we help them resolve the spiritual tensions they express?

These are the kinds of questions this guide seeks to answer. Its purpose is to help people who want to meet the spiritual needs of people in crisis. This is worked out through six weeks of daily Bible studies, each of which should take about thirty minutes. You need not follow the schedule of weeks and days; however, do the studies in the order given since they build on one another.

The first two weeks of studies set the context. Week one begins by considering our goals in providing spiritual care. Week two then covers what it means to be human and what God desires for his creatures. The next two weeks offer help in identifying spiritual needs (week three) and learning how to meet those needs (week four). The last two weeks consider the resources we can draw on as we care for those in crisis (week five) and the resources available to strengthen our own life with God (week six).

Each day's study has included the Scripture passage so you can feel free to mark them and write notes in the margins. You will need four colored markers to underline or circle different aspects of each passage. A notebook will also be necessary to record your responses to the questions. Before you begin each study, ask God to teach you from his Word.

Although studying these passages individually will be beneficial, studying them in a group will be even better. If you are not in such a group now, maybe you could start one. You can help each other understand God's Word better. You can pray for one another as you seek to live out his teaching. (Be sure to bring your notebooks to share your work from the week with each other.) There is a study concluding each week of daily studies to help guide group discussions. If you'd like more help in preparing and leading such a discussion, I recommend James Nyquist's helpful summary *Leading Bible Discussions* (IVP). Chapter eight might be especially useful.

The main outline of this book is correlated with *Spiritual Care: The Nurse's Role*. So *Caring in Crisis* can be a supplement to that book. But you need not be a nurse and you need not have read *Spiritual Care* to benefit from this guide. All you need is an openness to God's Spirit and a willingness to be a channel of love to people in need.

1
Responsible Caring

If we believe that people are created by God, in his image, and that a relationship with God is necessary for true health and fullness of life, then meeting spiritual needs must be an integral part of Christian caring. But spiritual care raises many questions in the minds of some people. Where do we get our mandate? What is our focus? How can we care for people spiritually when many of our friends and acquaintances are not Christians? Do they really want such care, or is their spiritual life a private matter?

The Bible gives us insight into God's will for us as responsible, caring persons. The following studies will consider some of God's answers to the questions above.

1 Day 1: **Our Mandate**

1 What is your mandate as a Christian? Who gives it to you? Isaiah 61:1-3 is the passage Jesus chose to read in the synagogue in Nazareth to announce the beginning of his earthly ministry (Lk. 4:18-19). As a Christian, with Christ in you, you are called to minister in his name. Read Isaiah 61:1-3 now.

2 Using markers of different colors, circle the answers to the following: (a) Who gives you your mandate for ministry (red)? (You may want to look up mandate in a dictionary.) (b) To whom are you called to minister (blue)? (c) What are you commissioned to do (green)? (d) What will the end result be (black)?

3 Think about each category of persons you circled in blue. Write down examples of people in each category whom you encounter. (For example, who are the brokenhearted people in your life?)

4 What is involved in each form of ministry you have circled in green? (For example, how can you "bind up" a person who is brokenhearted?)

5 Think of one person—a family member, a friend—who needs your ministry. What can you do for that person according to this passage?

6 What should be the end result of your intervention according to the passage?

The Spirit of the Lord GOD *is upon me,*
  because the LORD *has anointed me*
to bring good tidings to the afflicted;
  he has sent me to bind up the brokenhearted,
to proclaim liberty to the captives,
  and the opening of the prison to those who are bound;
to proclaim the year of the LORD's *favor,*
  and the day of vengeance of our God;
  to comfort all who mourn;
to grant to those who mourn in Zion—
  to give them a garland instead of ashes,
the oil of gladness instead of mourning,
  the mantle of praise instead of a faint spirit;
that they may be called oaks of righteousness,
  the planting of the LORD, *that he may be glorified.*
Isaiah 61:1-3

1 Day 2: **Our Focus**

1 Read Luke 10:1-12, 16-20. This scene took place early in Jesus' ministry as he trained his followers. Some of his specific instructions changed as his death on the cross drew nearer (compare Lk. 22:35-38), but his focus remained the same.

2 What was the ministry the seventy were appointed to perform?

3 Who were the people Jesus wanted them to go to?

4 Describe the environment they were to go out into.

5 Compare their situation with your environment where you live, work or go to school.

6 What would be the purpose of sending them out two by two?

7 What effect does the presence of another Christian in your environment have on you?

8 According to the passage, how does prayer change things?

9 Jesus instructed the seventy to stay in the same house, rather than move from house to house. What are some elements in a stable living situation which enhance a Christian's ability to reach out to others?

10 How much authority did Jesus give the seventy?

11 Along with the responsibility and authority to minister in his name, Jesus also gave them the power to carry out their mandate, but he reprimanded them when they became excited about that power. Why? Where does he want their focus to be?

12 What does it mean to "rejoice that your names are written in heaven"?

13 What mandate for ministry has God given you? Who are the people you have been called to serve?

After this the Lord appointed seventy others, and sent them on ahead of him, two by two, into every town and place where he himself was about to come. And he said to them, "The harvest is plentiful, but the laborers are few; pray therefore the Lord of the harvest to send out laborers into his harvest. Go your way; behold, I send you out as lambs in the midst of wolves. Carry no purse, no bag, no sandals; and salute no one on the road. Whatever house you enter, first say, 'Peace be to this house!' And if a son of peace is there, your peace shall rest upon him; but if not, it shall return to you. And remain in the same house, eating and drinking what they provide, for the laborer deserves his wages; do not go from house to house. Whenever you enter a town and they receive you, eat what is set before you; heal the sick in it and say to them, 'The kingdom of God has come near to you.' But whenever you enter a town and they do not receive you, go into its streets and say, 'Even the dust of your town that clings to our feet, we wipe off against you; nevertheless know this, that the kingdom of God has come near.' I tell you, it shall be more tolerable on that day for Sodom than for that town. . . .

"He who hears you hears me, and he who rejects you rejects me, and he who rejects me rejects him who sent me."

The seventy returned with joy, saying, "Lord, even the demons are subject to us in your name!" And he said to them, "I saw Satan fall like lightning from heaven. Behold, I have given you authority to tread upon serpents and scorpions, and over all the power of the enemy; and nothing shall hurt you. Nevertheless do not rejoice in this, that the spirits are subject to you; but rejoice that your names are written in heaven. Luke 10:1-12, 16-20

1 Day 3: **Being a Servant**

1 Foot washing, in Jesus' time, was a sign of hospitality. It was usually performed by a slave. What are some of the tasks which you might need to perform for people in crisis that would be the equivalent of foot washing?

2 Read John 13:1-17, 20. Jesus washed the feet of each disciple, including Judas. What implications does his example have for you?

3 What provides the Christian's motivation for being a servant to others?

4 What is the hardest part of being a servant for you?

5 Joanne is a nurse who feels that it is her responsibility as a Christian to go out of her way to care for patients cheerfully and compassionately. Recently she has noticed that other staff seem to be taking advantage of her willingness to serve. She has been assigned to all the patients requiring tedious care and constant attention. What would you do if you found yourself in her situation?

6 Reviewing the passages from this week we see that along with proclaiming the gospel, Jesus also expected his followers to minister to the physical needs of people they encountered. What does physical care have to do with meeting people's spiritual needs?

Now before the feast of the Passover, when Jesus knew that his hour had come to depart out of this world to the Father, having loved his own who were in the world, he loved them to the end. And during supper, when the devil had already put it into the heart of Judas Iscariot, Simon's son, to betray him, Jesus, knowing that the Father had given all things into his hands, and that he had come from God and was going to God, rose from supper, laid aside his garments, and girded himself with a towel. Then he poured water into a basin, and began to wash the disciples' feet, and to wipe them with the towel with which he was girded. He came to Simon Peter; and Peter said to him, "Lord, do you wash my feet?" Jesus answered him, "What I am doing you do not know now, but afterward you will understand." Peter said to him, "You shall never wash my feet." Jesus answered him, "If I do not wash you, you have no part in me." Simon Peter said to him, "Lord, not my feet only but also my hands and my head!" Jesus said to him, "He who has bathed does not need to wash, except for his feet, but he is clean all over; and you are clean, but not every one of you." For he knew who was to betray him; that was why he said, "You are not all clean."

When he had washed their feet, and taken his garments, and re-sumed his place, he said to them, "Do you know what I have done to you? You call me Teacher and Lord; and you are right, for so I am. If I then, your Lord and Teacher, have washed your feet, you also ought to wash one another's feet. For I have given you an example, that you also should do as I have done to you. Truly, truly, I say to you, a servant is not greater than his master; nor is he who is sent greater than he who sent him. If you know these things, blessed are you if you do them. . . . Truly, truly, I say to you, he who receives any one whom I send receives me; and he who receives me receives him who sent me." John 13:1-17, 20

1 Day 4: **Living in a Pluralistic World**

1 Read Colossians 2:2-19. (a) Underline all the phrases pertaining to Christ (red). (b) Underline all the phrases pertaining to you, as a believer (blue). (c) Put a check mark beside each attack of the world on Christian faith.

2 List each of the directives given in this passage. How does each apply in your situation?

3 In your own words, summarize who Jesus is and what he has done, according to this passage.

4 What effect has Jesus Christ had on your life?

5 The Colossians were influenced by both pagans and legalistic Jews. Local teachers were trying to convince them that certain beliefs and practices should be incorporated into their faith in Christ. List these various influences, beliefs or practices and write down a contemporary example of each you see in your own culture. (For example, false arguments—humanistic philosophy.)

6 Currently many philosophies and movements are popping up in a variety of guises that may appear to be scientifically proven (such as Transcendental Meditation or Yoga) but in reality are systems of thought based on beliefs about human nature, the nature of God and the universe that are inconsistent or contrary to the teachings of Scripture. How can what we know about Christ and what he has done for us help us to evaluate the world's teachings and philosophies?

7 What support does this passage give us for assessing and meeting spiritual needs of people in crisis?

*Christ himself . . . is the key that opens all the hidden treasures of God's
wisdom and knowledge.*

*I tell you, then, do not let anyone deceive you with false arguments, no
matter how good they seem to be. For even though I am absent in body,
yet I am with you in spirit, and I am glad as I see the resolute firmness
with which you stand together in your faith in Christ.*

*Since you have accepted Christ Jesus as Lord, live in union with him.
Keep your roots deep in him, build your lives on him, and become
stronger in your faith, as you were taught. And be filled with thanksgiving.*

*See to it, then, that no one enslaves you by means of the worthless
deceit of human wisdom, which comes from the teachings handed down
by men and from the ruling spirits of the universe, and not from Christ.
For the full content of divine nature lives in Christ, in his humanity, and
you have been given full life in union with him. He is supreme over every
spiritual ruler and authority. In union with Christ you were circumcised,
not with the circumcision that is made by men, but with the circumcision
made by Christ, which consists of being freed from the power of this sinful self. For when you were baptized, you were buried with Christ, and in
baptism you were also raised with Christ through your faith in the active
power of God, who raised him from death. You were at one time spiritually dead because of your sins and because you were Gentiles without
the Law. But God has now brought you to life with Christ. God forgave
us all our sins; he canceled the unfavorable record of our debts with its
binding rules and did away with it completely by nailing it to the cross.
And on that cross Christ freed himself from the power of the spiritual
rulers and authorities; he made a public spectacle of them by leading
them as captives in his victory procession.*

*So let no one make rules about what you eat or drink or about holy
days or the New Moon Festival or the Sabbath. All such things are only
a shadow of things in the future; the reality is Christ. Do not allow yourselves to be condemned by anyone who claims to be superior because of
special visions and who insists on false humility and the worship of
angels. For no reason at all, such a person is all puffed up by his human
way of thinking and has stopped holding on to Christ, who is the head of
the body. Under Christ's control the whole body is nourished and held
together by its joints and ligaments, and it grows as God wants it to grow.*
Colossians 2:2-19 (TEV)

1 Day 5: **The Religious Instinct**

1 Read Acts 17:16-34. What was the *initial* reaction of the Greek philosophers to Paul? What reaction followed his speech in the Areopagus?

2 Describe in your own words the Athenian society presented in this passage. How is our present-day society similar?

3 What clues to spiritual needs did Paul observe in Athens?

4 Outline Paul's message. What principles seemed to guide his presentation of the gospel to the Athenians?

5 Consider how you could use a person's interest in TM to tell him or her about Christ. Using Paul's principles, write down the way you might approach such a person.

6 What are the three different responses to Paul's message? How did Paul handle each?

7 What should we do when people do not respond positively to our attempts to meet their spiritual needs?

Now while Paul was waiting for them at Athens, his spirit was provoked within him as he saw that the city was full of idols. So he argued in the synagogue with the Jews and the devout persons, and in the market place every day with those who chanced to be there. Some also of the Epicurean and Stoic philosophers met him. And some said, "What would this babbler say?" Others said, "He seems to be a preacher of foreign divinities"—because he preached Jesus and the resurrection. And they took hold of him and brought him to the Areopagus, saying, "May we know what this new teaching is which you present? For you bring some strange things to our ears; we wish to know therefore what these things mean." Now all the Athenians and the foreigners who lived there spent their time in nothing except telling or hearing something new.

So Paul, standing in the middle of the Areopagus, said: "Men of Athens, I perceive that in every way you are very religious. For as I passed along, and observed the objects of your worship, I found also an altar with this inscription, 'To an unknown god.' What therefore you worship as unknown, this I proclaim to you. The God who made the world and everything in it, being Lord of heaven and earth, does not live in shrines made by man, nor is he served by human hands, as though he needed anything, since he himself gives to all men life and breath and everything. And he made from one every nation of men to live on all the face of the earth, having determined allotted periods and the boundaries of their habitation, that they should seek God, in the hope that they might feel after him and find him. Yet he is not far from each one of us, for

'In him we live and move and have our being';

as even some of your poets have said,

'For we are indeed his offspring.'

Being then God's offspring, we ought not to think that the Deity is like gold, or silver, or stone, a representation by the art and imagination of man. The times of ignorance God overlooked, but now he commands all men everywhere to repent, because he has fixed a day on which he will judge the world in righteousness by a man whom he has appointed, and of this he has given assurance to all men by raising him from the dead."

Now when they heard of the resurrection of the dead, some mocked; but others said, "We will hear you again about this." So Paul went out from among them. But some men joined him and believed, among them Dionysius the Areopagite and a woman named Damaris and others with them. Acts 17:16-34

1 Day 6: **A Dying Man Prays to God**

1 Read Isaiah 38:1-5, 9-20. What was Hezekiah's initial response when Isaiah said he was going to die? How did he pray?
2 How does God answer?
3 How would you account for the fact that God's answer did not exactly correspond with Hezekiah's prayer?
4 Notice that it was only in retrospect that Hezekiah could fluently describe his concerns. If you had been near him, what spiritual needs would you have discerned while he was ill? How would you have attempted to meet those needs?
5 What are Hezekiah's primary concerns as a dying man, described in his "writing"?
6 If you assume that Hezekiah's concerns are fairly common to dying people, what would be most helpful to them?

In those days Hezekiah became sick and was at the point of death. And Isaiah the prophet the son of Amoz came to him, and said to him, "Thus says the LORD: Set your house in order; for you shall die, you shall not recover." Then Hezekiah turned his face to the wall, and prayed to the LORD, and said, "Remember now, O LORD, I beseech thee, how I have walked before thee in faithfulness and with a whole heart, and have done what is good in thy sight." And Hezekiah wept bitterly. Then the word of the LORD came to Isaiah: "Go and say to Hezekiah, Thus says the LORD, the God of David your father: I have heard your prayer, I have seen your tears; behold, I will add fifteen years to your life. . . .

A writing of Hezekiah king of Judah, after he had been sick and had recovered from his sickness:
I said, In the noontide of my days
I must depart;
I am consigned to the gates of Sheol
for the rest of my years.
I said, I shall not see the LORD
in the land of the living;
I shall look upon man no more
among the inhabitants of the world.
My dwelling is plucked up and removed from me

like a shepherd's tent;
like a weaver I have rolled up my life;
*   he cuts me off from the loom;*
from day to night thou dost bring me to an end;
*   I cry for help until morning;*
like a lion he breaks all my bones;
*   from day to night thou dost bring me to an end.*

Like a swallow or a crane I clamor,
*   I moan like a dove.*
My eyes are weary with looking upward.
*   O Lord, I am oppressed; be thou my security!*
But what can I say? For he has spoken to me,
*   and he himself has done it.*
All my sleep has fled
*   because of the bitterness of my soul.*
O Lord, by these things men live,
*   and in all these is the life of my spirit.*
*   Oh, restore me to health and make me live!*
Lo, it was for my welfare
*   that I had great bitterness;*
but thou hast held back my life
*   from the pit of destruction,*
for thou has cast all my sins
*   behind thy back.*
For Sheol cannot thank thee,
*   death cannot praise thee;*
those who go down to the pit cannot hope
*   for thy faithfulness.*
the living, the living, he thanks thee,
*   as I do this day;*
the father makes known to the children
*   thy faithfulness.*

The LORD will save me,
*   and we will sing to stringed instruments*
all the days of our life,
*   at the house of the LORD.*
Isaiah 38:1-5, 9-20

1 Group Discussion: Responsible Caring

1 Review the kinds of people you studied in this week's passages that Christians are called to help.

2 Think about the people you spend most of your time with. Do any of them meet the above descriptions? How can you help them?

If you find that most of your associates are not "needy" people, where should you look to find people who need your help? Are there people around you who are being ignored, ridiculed or abandoned? Are there any Christian programs for ministering in nursing homes, hospitals, prisons or impoverished areas which you could participate in?

3 How does the gospel relate to the specific needs of the people mentioned in these passages?

4 What behavior of such people might give clues to their spiritual hunger?

5 Role play a couple of the following situations where a person may be expressing spiritual hunger through neediness. Several others can play the roles of helping persons. (Try to relate the gospel to this person's needs.) After each role play ask the group to evaluate the discussion that took place. How well did the helpers perceive and minister to the needs of the helped? How did the helpers feel about their intervention? How did the person helped feel about the assistance he or she received?

a) A friend has just flunked out of college.

b) An unmarried girl has just discovered she is pregnant.

c) An athlete's doctor has told him that recent injuries will prevent him from ever participating in sports again.

d) Your brother has just broken his engagement.

e) Your best friend's father has been laid off from his job.

f) A friend has just found out she has cancer.

2
What
Is
Human?

Our understanding of the nature of human
beings is basic to the way we treat others. The
biblical view is unique. We believe that
God created us to live in fellowship with
himself. We believe that he made us in his own
image and gave us responsibilities in the
world. We believe that God is deeply and
constantly involved in our lives. The following
studies will help you to examine these beliefs
and consider the difference they should make
in how you care for others.

2 Day 1: **Created in God's Image**

1 Read Genesis 1:26-28; 2:7-9, 15-25. (a) Underline the phrases that pertain to God's provision for people (red). (b) Underline human responsibilities (blue).

2 How does the creation of the man and the woman differ from the creation of animals?

3 According to the provisions God made for humans in this passage, what are some basic needs of people which were present at creation?

4 For what purposes did God create human beings?

5 Describe the relationship between God and people in this passage.

6 What is the connection between being created in God's image and likeness and having dominion over all the earth?

7 What is involved in having dominion?

8 For what specific additional purposes did God create woman? What responsibilities does God give her? How do her responsibilities differ from the man's?

9 What can we learn about God by looking at his image and likeness in people?

10 According to this passage, who are you?

Then God said, "Let us make man in our image, after our likeness; and let them have dominion over the fish of the sea, and over the birds of the air, and over the cattle, and over all the earth, and over every creeping thing that creeps upon the earth." So God created man in his own image, in the image of God he created him; male and female he created them. And God blessed them, and God said to them, "Be fruitful and multiply, and fill the earth and subdue it; and have dominion over the fish of the sea and over the birds of the air and over every living thing that moves upon the earth." ...

The LORD God formed man of dust from the ground, and breathed into his nostrils the breath of life; and man became a living being. And the LORD God planted a garden in Eden, in the east; and there he put the man whom he had formed. And out of the ground the LORD God made to grow every tree that is pleasant to the sight and good for food, the tree of life also in the midst of the garden, and the tree of the knowledge of good and evil.

The LORD God took the man and put him in the garden of Eden to till it and keep it. And the LORD God commanded the man, saying, "You may freely eat of every tree of the garden; but of the tree of the knowledge of good and evil you shall not eat, for in the day that you eat of it you shall die."

Then the LORD God said, "It is not good that the man should be alone; I will make him a helper fit for him." So out of the ground the LORD God formed every beast of the field and every bird of the air, and brought them to the man to see what he would call them; and whatever the man called every living creature, that was its name. The man gave names to all cattle, and to the birds of the air, and to every beast of the field; but for the man there was not found a helper fit for him. So the LORD God caused a deep sleep to fall upon the man, and while he slept took one of his ribs and closed up its place with flesh; and the rib which the LORD God had taken from the man he made into a woman and brought her to the man. Then the man said,

"This at last is bone of my bones
    and flesh of my flesh;
she shall be called Woman,
    because she was taken out of Man."

Therefore a man leaves his father and his mother and cleaves to his wife, and they become one flesh. And the man and his wife were both naked, and were not ashamed. Genesis 1:26-28, 2:7-9, 15-25

2 Day 2: **Disobedient Creatures**

1 Read Genesis 3:1-20. Compare what God said would happen if the man and woman ate from "the tree of the knowledge of good and evil" (Gen. 2:9, 16-17) with what the serpent said would happen. In what way did both predictions come true? What was wrong with the serpent's prediction?

2 When the woman used her reason, what did she conclude about the fruit? What current ethical dilemmas are being dealt with in a similar manner in our society (that is, where has behavior which is forbidden by God become socially acceptable and attractive)? Why is human reason alone inadequate for ethical decision making?

3 The first result of eating the forbidden fruit is that the husband and wife were embarrassed because they were naked before each other and God. What does this indicate about the way sin changed their self-concepts?

4 How did their guilt affect their relationship with God? With each other?

5 What changes does God make in their lifestyle?

6 In what ways do their responsibilities, relationships and purposes in life remain the same?

7 What do you think is the significance of God making clothes for Adam and Eve?

8 If a Christian asked you, "Why do you pray with Sandy? She's not a Christian. You know God turns a deaf ear to unsaved people," how would you respond in the light of this passage alone?

Now the serpent was more subtle than any other wild creature that the LORD God had made. He said to the woman, "Did God say, 'You shall not eat of any tree of the garden'?" And the woman said to the serpent, "We may eat of the fruit of the trees of the garden; but God said, 'You shall not eat of the fruit of the tree which is in the midst of the garden, neither shall you touch it, lest you die.' " But the serpent said to the woman, "You will not die. For God knows that when you eat of it your eyes will be opened, and you will be like God, knowing good and evil." So when the woman saw that the tree was good for food, and that it was a delight to the eyes, and that the tree was to be desired to make one wise, she took of its fruit and ate; and she also gave some to her husband, and he ate. Then the eyes of both were opened, and they knew that they were naked; and they sewed fig leaves together and made themselves aprons.

And they heard the sound of the LORD God walking in the garden in the cool of the day, and the man and his wife hid themselves from the presence of the LORD God among the trees of the garden. But the LORD God called to the man, and said to him, "Where are you?" And he said, "I heard the sound of thee in the garden, and I was afraid, because I was naked; and I hid myself." He said, "Who told you that you were naked? Have you eaten of the tree of which I commanded you not to eat?" The man said, "The woman whom thou gavest to be with me, she gave me fruit of the tree, and I ate." Then the LORD God said to the woman, "What is this that you have done?" The woman said, "The serpent beguiled me, and I ate." The LORD God said to the serpent, "Because you have done this, cursed are you above all cattle, and above all wild animals; upon your belly you shall go, and dust you shall eat all the days of your life. I will put enmity between you and the woman, and between your seed and her seed; he shall bruise your head, and you shall bruise his heel." To the woman he said, "I will greatly multiply your pain in childbearing; in pain you shall bring forth children, yet your desire shall be for your husband, and he shall rule over you." And to Adam he said, "Because you have listened to the voice of your wife, and have eaten of the tree of which I commanded you, 'You shall not eat of it,' cursed is the ground because of you; in toil you shall eat of it all the days of your life; thorns and thistles it shall bring forth to you; and you shall eat the plants of the field. In the sweat of your face you shall eat bread till you return to the ground, for out of it you were taken; you are dust, and to dust you shall return."

The man called his wife's name Eve, because she was the mother of all living. And the LORD God made for Adam and for his wife garments of skins, and clothed them. Genesis 3:1-20

2 Day 3: **Known by God**

1 Read Psalm 139. In what areas of life does the psalmist see God involved? How did the psalmist find out these things about God?
2 At one point the psalmist seems to want to run from God. Have you ever felt like that? Why? In the second paragraph, what conclusions did the psalmist come to through this experience?
3 Close your eyes and think about darkness and light. What difference does it make that "night is as bright as the day" to God?
4 Note the verb tenses in the passage. What time span is covered? How was God active in the psalmist's past? What difference should it make for you to know that God has been in control of your development, including what you see as negative?
5 How does the psalmist describe the wicked? Contrast their attitude toward God with his attitude as described in the last verses.
6 List in a column the attributes of God illustrated in this psalm. Next to each attribute list the ways the psalmist was affected by this knowledge. What progression do you notice in his self-concept? What factors influence this change?
7 What does this knowledge about God cause you to see in yourself? Is there something that needs changing? Are there things you need to begin praising God for?

O LORD, thou hast searched me and known me!
Thou knowest when I sit down and when I rise up;
thou discernest my thoughts from afar.
Thou searchest out my path and my lying down,
and art acquainted with all my ways.
Even before a word is on my tongue,
lo, O LORD, thou knowest it altogether.
Thou dost beset me behind and before,
and layest thy hand upon me.
Such knowledge is too wonderful for me;
it is high, I cannot attain it.

Whither shall I go from thy Spirit?

Or whither shall I flee from thy presence?
If I ascend to heaven, thou art there!
 If I make my bed in Sheol, thou art there!
If I take the wings of the morning
 and dwell in the uttermost parts of the sea,
even there thy hand shall lead me,
 and thy right hand shall hold me.
If I say, "Let only darkness cover me,
 and the light about me be night,"
even the darkness is not dark to thee,
 the night is bright as the day; for darkness is as light with thee.

For thou didst form my inward parts,
 thou didst knit me together in my mother's womb.
I praise thee, for thou art fearful and wonderful.
Wonderful are thy works!
Thou knowest me right well;
 my frame was not hidden from thee,
when I was being made in secret,
 intricately wrought in the depths of the earth.
Thy eyes beheld my unformed substance;
 in thy book were written, every one of them,
the days that were formed for me,
 when as yet there was none of them.
How precious to me are thy thoughts, O God!
 How vast is the sum of them!
If I would count them, they are more than the sand.
 When I awake, I am still with thee.

O that thou wouldst slay the wicked, O God,
 and that men of blood would depart from me,
men who maliciously defy thee,
 who lift themselves up against thee for evil!
Do I not hate them that hate thee, O LORD?
 And do I not loathe them that rise up against thee?
I hate them with perfect hatred; I count them my enemies.
Search me, O God, and know my heart!
 Try me and know my thoughts!
And see if there be any wicked way in me,
 and lead me in the way everlasting! Psalm 139

2 Day 4: **An Integrated Whole**

1 Read Psalm 32. (a) Underline all the phrases pertaining to spiritual needs and activities (green). (b) Underline physical symptoms (red). (c) Underline expressions of emotion (blue). Identify each in the margin (for example, joy, fear, depression).
2 What happens to you physically and emotionally when you have done something you know is wrong?
3 What steps to forgiveness and healing does the psalmist advocate and demonstrate?
4 What does "constant love" involve according to this passage? How does God's "constant love" enable a person to cope with suffering?
5 Why does the psalmist advocate rejoicing? Summarize what he says God has done. What effect does rejoicing have on a person physically and psychosocially?
6 Each person "is a physically, psychosocially and spiritually integrated being created to live in harmony with God, himself and his environment" (Fish and Shelly, *Spiritual Care*, IVP, p. 33). How does Psalm 32 support this definition?

Happy are those whose sins are forgiven,
  whose wrongs are pardoned.
Happy is the man whom the LORD does not accuse of doing wrong
  and who is free from all deceit.
When I did not confess my sins,
  I was worn out from crying all day long.
Day and night you punished me, LORD;
  my strength was completely drained,
  as moisture is dried up by the summer heat.

Then I confessed my sins to you;
  I did not conceal my wrongdoings.
I decided to confess them to you,
  and you forgave all my sins.

So all your loyal people should pray to you in times of need;
  when a great flood of trouble comes rushing in,
  it will not reach them.
You are my hiding place;
  you will save me from trouble.
I sing aloud of your salvation,
  because you protect me.

The LORD says, "I will teach you the way you should go;
  I will instruct you and advise you.
Don't be stupid like a horse or a mule,
  which must be controlled with a bit and bridle
  to make it submit."

The wicked will have to suffer,
  but those who trust in the LORD
  are protected by his constant love.
You that are righteous, be glad and rejoice
  because of what the LORD has done.
You that obey him, shout for joy!
Psalm 32 (TEV)

2 Day 5: **Loved and Formed by God**

1 Read Isaiah 43:1-13. (a) Circle all the names of God (red). (b) Underline all the phrases describing God's activity (red). (c) Circle all the terms referring to God's people (blue). (d) Underline the phrases describing the activities, responsibilities and condition of God's people (blue).

2 Describe God's relationship to his people. What has he done for them?

3 What function is God's people given to perform in the world?

4 This chapter was probably written during the Babylonian captivity. On what basis does he tell them to "fear not"? What does he promise them?

5 How could you use this passage to bring comfort and hope to someone who was suffering? Think through the significance of each of the things described in this passage that God does for his people. How would it apply to those (don't forget yourself!) who are not able to see hope in their (or your) present situation?

But now thus says the LORD,
he who created you, O Jacob,
　he who formed you, O Israel:
"Fear not, for I have redeemed you;
　I have called you by name, you are mine.
When you pass through the waters I will be with you;
　and through the rivers, they shall not overwhelm you;
　when you walk through fire you shall not be burned,
　and the flame shall not consume you.
For I am the LORD your God,
　the Holy One of Israel, your Savior.
I give Egypt as your ransom,

Ethiopia and Seba in exchange for you.
Because you are precious in my eyes,
    and honored, and I love you,
I give men in return for you,
    peoples in exchange for your life.
Fear not, for I am with you;
    I will bring your offspring from the east,
    and from the west I will gather you;
I will say to the north, Give up,
    and to the south, Do not withhold;
bring my sons from afar
    and my daughters from the end of the earth,
every one who is called by my name,
whom I created for my glory,
whom I formed and made."

Bring forth the people who are blind, yet have eyes,
    who are deaf, yet have ears!
Let all the nations gather together,
    and let the peoples assemble.
Who among them can declare this,
    and show us the former things?
Let them bring their witnesses to justify them,
    and let them hear and say, It is true.
"You are my witnesses," says the LORD,
    "and my servant whom I have chosen,
that you may know and believe me
    and understand that I am He.
Before me no god was formed,
    nor shall there be any after me.
I, I am the LORD,
    and besides me there is no savior.
I declared and saved and proclaimed,
    when there was no strange god among you;
    and you are my witnesses," says the LORD.
"I am God, and also henceforth I am He;
    there is none who can deliver from my hand;
    I work and who can hinder it?"
Isaiah 43:1-13

2 Day 6: **Redeemed by God**

1 Read Romans 1. (a) Circle any frequently repeated words or phrases. (b) Underline the key verses in the chapter.

2 How does Paul introduce himself to the Romans? In what ways does his relationship with God establish his authority and identity?

3 Compare Paul's description of himself to the way you would introduce yourself to a new group of people.

4 What reasons does Paul give for wanting to see the Romans?

5 What is the gospel according to this passage?

6 What basic sin is the object of God's wrath? What punishment does God give to those who disobey him?

7 How does this basic sin affect a person's: (a) self-concept and personal sense of identity? (b) interpersonal relationships? (c) ability to reason? (d) attitude toward life in general?

8 Contrast the answers above with Paul's self-concept, interpersonal relationships, ability to reason and attitude toward life.

9 What difference has the gospel made in your life?

Paul, a servant of Jesus Christ, called to be an apostle, set apart for the gospel of God which he promised beforehand through his prophets in the holy scriptures, the gospel concerning his Son, who was descended from David according to the flesh and designated Son of God in power according to the Spirit of holiness by his resurrection from the dead, Jesus Christ our Lord, through whom we have received grace and apostleship to bring about the obedience of faith for the sake of his name among all the nations, including yourselves who are called to belong to Jesus Christ;

To all God's beloved in Rome, who are called to be saints:

Grace to you and peace from God our Father and the Lord Jesus Christ.

First, I thank my God through Jesus Christ for all of you, because your faith is proclaimed in all the world. For God is my witness, whom I serve with my spirit in the gospel of his Son, that without ceasing I mention you always in my prayers, asking that somehow by God's will I may now at last succeed in coming to you. For I long to see you, that I may impart to you some spiritual gift to strengthen you, that is, that we may be mutually encouraged by each other's faith, both yours and mine. I want you to know, brethren, that I have often intended to come to you (but thus far have been prevented), in order that I may reap some harvest among you as well as among the rest of the Gentiles. I am under obligation both to Greeks and to barbarians, both to the wise and to the foolish: so I am eager to preach the gospel to you also who are in Rome.

For I am not ashamed of the gospel: it is the power of God for salvation to every one who has faith, to the Jew first and also to the Greek. For in it the righteousness of God is revealed through faith for faith; as it is written, "He who through faith is righteous shall live."

For the wrath of God is revealed from heaven against all ungodliness and wickedness of men who by their wickedness suppress the truth. For what can be known about God is plain to them, because God has shown it to them. Ever since the creation of the world his invisible nature, namely, his eternal power and deity, has been clearly perceived in the things that have been made. So they are without excuse; for although they knew God they did not honor him as God or give thanks to him, but they became futile in their thinking and their senseless minds were darkened. Claiming to be wise, they became fools, and exchanged the glory of the immortal God for images resembling mortal man or birds or animals or reptiles.

Therefore God gave them up in the lusts of their hearts to impurity, to the dishonoring of their bodies among themselves, because they exchanged the truth about God for a lie and worshiped and served the creature rather than the Creator, who is blessed for ever! Amen.

For this reason God gave them up to dishonorable passions. Their women exchanged natural relations for unnatural, and the men likewise gave up natural relations with women and were consumed with passion for one another, men committing shameless acts with men and receiving in their own persons the due penalty for their error.

And since they did not see fit to acknowledge God, God gave them up to a base mind and to improper conduct. They were filled with all manner of wickedness, evil, covetousness, malice. Full of envy, murder, strife, deceit, malignity, they are gossips, slanderers, haters of God, insolent, haughty, boastful, inventors of evil, disobedient to parents, foolish, faithless, heartless, ruthless. Though they know God's decree that those who do such things deserve to die, they not only do them but approve those who practice them. Romans 1

2 Group Discussion: What Is Human?

1 What implications does the fact that all human beings are created in the image of God have on the way we should relate to others?

2 What does "having dominion" mean to you? How is it related to your daily life?

3 In what specific ways do you see the effects of sin in your own life and in the world around you?

4 Discuss question 8 from day two (Gen. 3:1-20). How did you answer the question? On what basis?

5 What does it mean to you (for example, in terms of self-concept, motivation, meaning and purpose, attitudes toward others and so on) to have God active in your life from the time of conception?

6 In what ways have you seen the interrelationship between your emotions, your physical health and your relationship to God in your life?

7 How does the gospel of Jesus Christ make us more fully human?

3
Identifying Spiritual Needs

People need help to establish or maintain a
dynamic relationship with God. Such
spiritual needs are manifested in several areas.
The need for meaning and purpose, the
need for love and relationships with others,
and the need for forgiveness are examples
of spiritual needs because they are rooted in a
basic need for a relationship with God.
Everyone has spiritual needs—the helper and
the helped, Christians and non-Christians.
God often uses people to continually draw
us to himself.

3 Day 1: **The Need for Meaning and Purpose**

1 What gives your life meaning and purpose?

2 Read the passages from 1 Peter. How does Peter address the recipients of his letter? In what ways does his salutation define their meaning and purpose in life?

3 What does this passage say about the meaning and purpose of: (a) salvation (new life); (b) suffering; (c) faith. Note: "your souls" might be better translated "yourselves."

4 According to this passage, what is involved in holy living?

5 How can an awareness of our meaning and purpose in life affect our ability and desire to lead a holy life?

6 Toward the end of chapter 1, Peter exhorts the believers to "love one another earnestly with all your heart," after telling them that they have already "come to a sincere love for" their fellow believers. What else might have been needed to fulfill this exhortation?

7 Give percentage estimates on how you spend your waking hours (in work, play, study, meals, other). How is your meaning and purpose in life demonstrated in your behavior? What areas do you need to work on?

From Peter, apostle of Jesus Christ—

to God's chosen people who live as refugees scattered throughout the provinces of Pontus, Galatia, Cappadocia, Asia, and Bithynia. You were chosen according to the purpose of God the Father and were made a holy people by his Spirit, to obey Jesus Christ and be purified by his blood.

May grace and peace be yours in full measure.

Let us give thanks to the God and Father of our Lord Jesus Christ! Because of his great mercy he gave us new life by raising Jesus Christ from death. This fills us with a living hope, and so we look forward to possessing the rich blessings that God keeps for his people. He keeps them for you in heaven, where they cannot decay or spoil or fade away. They are for you, who through faith are kept safe by God's power for the salvation which is ready to be revealed at the end of time.

Be glad about this, even though it may now be necessary for you to be sad for a while because of the many kinds of trials you suffer. Their purpose is to prove that your faith is genuine. Even gold, which can be destroyed, is tested by fire; and so your faith, which is much more precious than gold, must also be tested, so that it may endure. Then you will receive praise and glory and honor on the Day when Jesus Christ is revealed. You love him, although you have not seen him, and you believe in him, although you do not now see him. So you rejoice with a great and glorious joy which words cannot express, because you are receiving the salvation of your souls, which is the purpose of your faith in him. It was concerning this salvation that the prophets made careful search and investigation, and they prophesied about this gift which God would give you. They tried to find out when the time would be and how it would come. This was the time to which Christ's Spirit in them was pointing, in predicting the sufferings that Christ would have to endure and the glory that would follow. God revealed to these prophets that their work was not for their own benefit, but for yours, as they spoke about those things which you have now heard from the messengers who announced the Good News by the power of the Holy Spirit sent from heaven. These are things which even the angels would like to understand.

So then, have your minds ready for action. Keep alert and set your hope completely on the blessing which will be given you when Jesus Christ is revealed. Be obedient to God, and do not allow your lives to be shaped by those desires you had when you were still ignorant. Instead, be holy in all that you do, just as God who called you is holy. The scripture says, "Be holy because I am holy." . . .

Now that by your obedience to the truth you have purified yourselves and have come to have a sincere love for your fellow believers, love one another earnestly with all your heart. For through the living and eternal word of God you have been born again as the children of a parent who is immortal, not mortal.

As the Scripture says,
"All mankind are like grass,
    and all their glory is like wild flowers.
The grass withers, and the flowers fall,
    but the word of the Lord remains forever."
This word is the Good News that was proclaimed to you.
1 Peter 1:1-16, 22-25 (TEV)

3 Day 2: **The Source of Meaning and Purpose**

1 Read both Psalm 8 and Ecclesiastes 1:1-15. (a) Underline everything pertaining to the human race (red). (b) Underline phrases pertaining to creation (green). (c) Underline references to God (blue).

2 Describe the tone in each passage (for example, open, businesslike, calm and so on).

3 What does each writer see as the human task in life?

4 Describe the relationship of mankind to creation in each passage. How does this relationship affect each writer's sense of meaning and purpose?

5 Describe each writer's view of God. How does it influence his meaning and purpose in life?

6 Which writer do you identify with most, the psalmist or the preacher? Explain.

7 How does a personal relationship with God provide meaning and purpose in life for you?

8 In what ways could you communicate meaning and purpose to cynical people?

O LORD, our Lord,
how majestic is thy name in all the earth!

Thou whose glory above the heavens is chanted
    by the mouth of babes and infants,
thou hast founded a bulwark because of thy foes,
    to still the enemy and the avenger.

When I look at thy heavens, the work of thy fingers,

the moon and the stars which thou hast established;
what is man that thou art mindful of him,
    and the son of man that thou dost care for him?

Yet thou has made him little less than God,
    and dost crown him with glory and honor.
Thou hast given him dominion over the works of thy hands;
    thou hast put all things under his feet,
all sheep and oxen,
    and also the beasts of the field,
the birds of the air, and the fish of the sea,
    whatever passes along the paths of the sea.

O LORD, our Lord,
    how majestic is thy name in all the earth!
Psalm 8

The words of the Preacher, the son of David, king in Jerusalem.
Vanity of vanities, says the Preacher, vanity of vanities! All is vanity. What
does man gain by all the toil at which he toils under the sun? A generation
goes, and a generation comes, but the earth remains for ever. The sun
rises and the sun goes down, and hastens to the place where it rises. The
wind blows to the south, and goes round to the north; round and round
goes the wind, and on its circuits the wind returns. All streams run to the
sea, but the sea is not full; to the place where the streams flow, there they
flow again. All things are full of weariness; a man cannot utter it; the eye is
not satisfied with seeing, nor the ear filled with hearing. What has been is
what will be, and what has been done is what will be done; and there is
nothing new under the sun. Is there a thing of which it is said, "See, this
is new"? It has been already, in the ages before us. There is no remem-
brance of former things, nor will there be any remembrance of later things
yet to happen among those who come after.

I the Preacher have been king over Israel in Jerusalem. And I applied
my mind to seek and to search out by wisdom all that is done under
heaven; it is an unhappy business that God has given to the sons of men
to be busy with. I have seen everything that is done under the sun; and
behold, all is vanity and a striving after wind. What is crooked cannot be
made straight, and what is lacking cannot be numbered. Ecclesiastes
1:1-15

3 Day 3: **The Source of Love**

1 Read 1 John 4:7-21. (a) Circle *love, loves* and *loved* each time they appear. (b) Underline the key verse.

2 What is love according to these verses?

3 What is the source of love?

4 How do we experience that love, according to John? What effects does he say love has on us?

5 What enables us to love other people?

6 How does love drive out fear? Can you think of an example in your life where this happened?

7 Is there anything that frightens you now? If so, how could love change things? Who would do the loving? Who would the love be directed toward? In what ways could love be expressed?

8 What would you do if someone in a crisis situation was so annoying that you felt that you could not love that person?

Dear friends, let us love one another, because love comes from God. Whoever loves is a child of God and knows God. Whoever does not love does not know God, for God is love. And God showed his love for us by sending his only Son into the world, so that we might have life through him. This is what love is: it is not that we have loved God, but that he loved us and sent his Son to be the means by which our sins are forgiven.

Dear friends, if this is how God loved us, then we should love one another. No one has ever seen God, but if we love one another, God lives in union with us, and his love is made perfect in us.

We are sure that we live in union with God and that he lives in union with us, because he has given us his Spirit. And we have seen and tell others that the Father sent his Son to be the Savior of the world. If anyone declares that Jesus is the Son of God, he lives in union with God and God lives in union with him. And we ourselves know and believe the love which God has for us.

God is love, and whoever lives in love lives in union with God and God lives in union with him. Love is made perfect in us in order that we may have courage on the Judgment Day; and we will have it because our life in this world is the same as Christ's. There is no fear in love; perfect love drives out all fear. So then, love has not been made perfect in anyone who is afraid, because fear has to do with punishment.

We love because God first loved us. If someone says he loves God, but hates his brother, he is a liar. For he cannot love God, whom he has not seen, if he does not love his brother, whom he has seen. The Command that Christ has given us is this: whoever loves God must love his brother also. 1 John 4:7-21 (TEV)

3 Day 4: **The Meaning of Love**

1 Hosea was a prophet in Israel. At the beginning of his prophetic career God told him to marry a prostitute. Hosea's life with his unfaithful wife became a parallel of God's relationship to Israel. Read Hosea 11. (a) Underline God's feelings and actions toward Israel (red). Note: Ephraim is an earlier name for the land included in the kingdom of Israel. (b) Underline Israel's responses to God (green).

2 Examine the ways God expresses his love for Israel in this passage. Compile a definition of love based on your observations. (For example, God loved Israel as a child and called him out of Egypt; therefore, you might conclude that love includes freeing a person from bondage.

3 What does Israel's response to God's love indicate about its primary concerns?

4 Why did Israel continually reject God's love?

5 How does rebellion affect a person's ability to perceive and receive love?

6 Why does God express anger toward Israel? How is God's anger related to his love?

7 According to this passage, what is the primary characteristic of love? In what ways could you demonstrate this characteristic?

When Israel was a child, I loved him,
and out of Egypt I called my son.
The more I called them,
the more they went from me;
they kept sacrificing to the Baals,
and burning incense to idols.

Yet it was I who taught Ephraim to walk,
I took them up in my arms;
but they did not know that I healed them.
I led them with cords of compassion,

with the bands of love,
and I became to them as one
  who eases the yoke on their jaws,
  and I bent down to them and fed them.

They shall return to the land of Egypt,
  and Assyria shall be their king,
  because they have refused to return to me.
The sword shall rage against their cities,
  consume the bars of their gates,
  and devour them in their fortresses.
My people are bent on turning away from me;
  so they are appointed to the yoke,
  and none shall remove it.

How can I give you up, O Ephraim!
  How can I hand you over, O Israel!
How can I make you like Admah!
  How can I treat you like Zeboiim!
My heart recoils within me,
  my compassion grows warm and tender.
I will not execute my fierce anger,
  I will not again destroy Ephraim;
for I am God and not man,
  the Holy One in your midst,
  and I will not come to destroy.

They shall go after the LORD,
  he will roar like a lion;
yea, he will roar,
  and his sons shall come trembling from the west;
they shall come trembling like birds from Egypt,
  and like doves from the land of Assyria;
  and I will return them to their homes, says the LORD.
Ephraim has encompassed me with lies,
  and the house of Israel with deceit;
but Judah is still known by God,
  and is faithful to the Holy One.
Hosea 11

3 Day 5: **Our Need for Forgiveness**

1 Read 1 John 1:1—2:2. (a) Give a title to each paragraph of the passage. (b) Circle key words that are frequently repeated (using a different color for each word).

2 What is the Word John is referring to in the first paragraph?

3 What is the relationship between Christian fellowship and joy?

4 Imagine that you are in a strange, dark room and you want to walk across it. What difficulties might you encounter?

5 Now imagine that someone turns on the light. What difference does that make? What does John mean when he says, "God is light"? What does it mean for us to "live in the light"?

6 How does living in the light result in fellowship?

7 How does living in the light enable us to confess our sin?

8 Why is confession of sin so important?

9 Spend a few minutes examining your attitudes and behavior over the past week. Expose them to the light of God and confess what God reveals to you as sin.

10 If you are struggling with nagging guilt over things in your past, confess them to God now, trusting him to keep his promise to forgive.

We write to you about the Word of life, which has existed from the very beginning. We have heard it, and we have seen it with our eyes; yes, we have seen it, and our hands have touched it. When this life became visible, we saw it; so we speak of it and tell you about the eternal life which was with the Father and was made known to us. What we have seen and heard we announce to you also, so that you will join with us in the fellowship that we have with the Father and with his Son Jesus Christ. We write this in order that our joy may be complete.

Now the message that we have heard from his Son and announce is this: God is light, and there is no darkness at all in him. If, then, we say that we have fellowship with him, yet at the same time live in the darkness, we are lying both in our words and in our actions. But if we live in the light—just as he is in the light—then we have fellowship with one another, and the blood of Jesus, his Son, purifies us from every sin.

If we say that we have no sin, we deceive ourselves, and there is no truth in us. But if we confess our sins to God, he will keep his promise and do what is right: he will forgive us our sins and purify us from all our wrongdoing. If we say that we have not sinned, we make a liar out of God, and his word is not in us.

I am writing this to you, my children, so that you will not sin; but if anyone does sin, we have someone who pleads with the Father on our behalf—Jesus Christ, the righteous one. And Christ himself is the means by which our sins are forgiven, and not our sins only, but also the sins of everyone. 1 John 1:1—2:2 (TEV)

3 Day 6: **The Way of Forgiveness**

1 How would you feel if you were teaching a Sunday-school class when the pastor came into the room and began quizzing you about your knowledge of the Bible in front of the class? How would you be tempted to respond?

2 Read John 8:1-11. What was Jesus doing when the Scribes and Pharisees arrived?

3 What was their motivation for interrupting him with their question?

4 How did Jesus respond to the Scribes and Pharisees?

5 What is the point of his answer to them?

6 Does Jesus condone sin by his statement to the woman?

7 What does forgiveness entail, according to this passage? What did the woman have to do to obtain it?

8 Consider what you would do in the following situation: A friend, Ted, is admitted to a hospital with a severe case of infectious hepatitis due to drug abuse. A mutual friend, Rose, comments to you, "He got himself into this situation—he can just suffer the consequences! He's not getting any sympathy from me."

They went each to his own house, but Jesus went to the Mount of Olives. Early in the morning he came again to the temple; all the people came to him, and he sat down and taught them. The scribes and the Pharisees brought a woman who had been caught in adultery, and placing her in the midst they said to him, "Teacher, this woman has been caught in the act of adultery. Now in the law Moses commanded us to stone such. What do you say about her?" This they said to test him, that they might have some charge to bring against him. Jesus bent down and wrote with his finger on the ground. And as they continued to ask him, he stood up and said to them, "Let him who is without sin among you be the first to throw a stone at her." And once more he bent down and wrote with his finger on the ground. But when they heard it, they went away, one by one, beginning with the eldest, and Jesus was left alone with the woman standing before him. Jesus looked up and said to her, "Woman, where are they? Has no one condemned you?" She said, "No one, Lord." And Jesus said, "Neither do I condemn you; go, and do not sin again."
John 8:1-11

3 Group Discussion: Identifying Spiritual Needs

1 Write on a piece of paper the three most important things in your life (including people and relationships, goals and accomplishments). Share what you wrote with the group and tell how each of these things gives you meaning and purpose in life.

2 At what point in your personal history did life seem most meaningless? What changed those feelings? How were other people helpful (or unhelpful) to you? Was any passage of Scripture particularly significant?

3 Who (besides God) has been the most loving person in your life? How was that love communicated? How has it made you feel?

4 Think of the person you love least. (You need not name who it is to the group.) What can you do to change your attitude toward this person? Discuss some ways you could act lovingly toward him or her. Stop and pray conversationally for a few minutes: (a) confessing unloving attitudes; (b) asking God to help one another.

5 As you confessed your sin of being unloving, you experienced God's forgiveness. What does being forgiven mean to you?

6 Discuss your answers to day six, question 8.

4
Meeting
Spiritual
Needs

You have a friend in a crisis who shows
evidence of certain spiritual needs. How can
you be sure such is the case? And even
if you are sure, what would you do next? What
would be the best way to help? Seldom is
there an obvious set of symptoms of spiritual
need. Making a proper assessment requires
a sensitive ear and a willingness to respond to
tiny clues.

4 Day 1: **Setting Priorities**

1 Read Luke 10: 25-42. Why does the lawyer approach Jesus? How does Jesus answer his initial question?

2 Explain the lawyer's response. What does his additional question reveal about his understanding of the law he quoted?

3 The robbers, priest, Levite and Samaritan each encountered the wounded man. What may have motivated the action of each toward him? In what ways are we motivated by similar things in our responses to people?

4 List each of the Samaritan's actions toward the wounded man. How does each action demonstrate love? What did each action cost him personally?

5 How was his total person involved (that is, heart, soul, mind, strength)? What did this have to do with loving God?

6 Think of the most unlovely (for example, physically repulsive, disagreeable, ungrateful) person in need that you ever met. Did you respond as the robber, priest, Levite or Samaritan? How could you have begun to implement God's love as the Samaritan did?

7 In the last paragraph, whom do you identify with—Mary or Martha? Why?

8 What do Martha's comments and actions reveal about her attitude toward Mary? Jesus? Herself?

9 Why did Jesus say that Mary had done the better thing? What does this show about Mary's sensitivity to Jesus' needs?

10 When guests visit you, what is communicated by much busyness? What can be accomplished by being still and listening? How does this apply to your relationship with God?

11 The Samaritan showed love by physical action, Mary showed it by listening. How can you determine which would take priority in a given situation? Think of specific situations at work and at home where you need to re-evaluate your priorities in order to show love.

And behold, a lawyer stood up to put him to the test, saying, "Teacher, what shall I do to inherit eternal life?" He said to him, "What is written in the law? How do you read?" And he answered, "You shall love the Lord your God with all your heart, and with all your soul, and with all your strength, and with all your mind; and your neighbor as yourself." And he said to him, "You have answered right; do this, and you will live."

But he, desiring to justify himself, said to Jesus, "And who is my neighbor?" Jesus replied, "A man was going down from Jerusalem to Jericho and he fell among robbers, who stripped him and beat him, and departed, leaving him half dead. Now by chance a priest was going down that road; and when he saw him he passed by on the other side. So likewise a Levite, when he came to the place and saw him, passed by on the other side. But a Samaritan, as he journeyed, came to where he was; and when he saw him, he had compassion, and went to him and bound up his wounds, pouring on oil and wine; then he set him on his own beast and brought him to an inn, and took care of him. And the next day he took out two denarii and gave them to the innkeeper, saying, 'Take care of him; and whatever more you spend, I will repay you when I come back.' Which of these three, do you think, proved neighbor to the man who fell among the robbers?" He said, "The one who showed mercy on him." And Jesus said to him, "Go and do likewise."

Now as they went on their way, he entered a village; and a woman named Martha received him into her house. And she had a sister called Mary, who sat at the Lord's feet and listened to his teaching. But Martha was distracted with much serving; and she went to him and said, "Lord, do you not care that my sister has left me to serve alone? Tell her then to help me." But the Lord answered her, "Martha, Martha, you are anxious and troubled about many things; one thing is needful. Mary has chosen the good portion, which shall not be taken away from her." Luke 10:25-42

4 Day 2: **A Psalmist's View of His Spiritual Needs**

1 Read Psalm 38. What does the psalmist see as the reason for his suffering? How does he view his sin?

2 What physical symptoms does he exhibit? (Some commentators think that he may have had leprosy.)

3 What emotional responses accompany his illness? How has his illness affected his self-concept?

4 How does the psalmist perceive his friends and family? His enemies? God? Why do you think he felt as he did?

5 List all of the psalmist's expressed needs (physical, emotional and spiritual) in the left-hand column. In the right-hand column consider what you could do to meet those needs.

Needs	Meeting the Needs
Ex: Lack of supportive people	*Spend time listening and encouraging. Ask family to visit.*

6 If this were someone you knew and you saw only the physical and emotional manifestations of illness, what questions would you ask to determine if there were any underlying spiritual needs? If you identified the need for forgiveness, how could you begin to meet this need?

7 Have you ever experienced anything of what the psalmist describes? How has your experience helped you to understand what someone else may feel?

8 What would you say are your own spiritual needs right now? How could they be met?

O LORD, rebuke me not in thy anger,
  nor chasten me in thy wrath!
For thy arrows have sunk into me,
  and thy hand has come down on me.

There is no soundness in my flesh because of thy indignation;
  there is no health in my bones because of my sin.
For my iniquities have gone over my head;
  they weigh like a burden too heavy for me.
My wounds grow foul and fester
  because of my foolishness,
I am utterly bowed down and prostrate;
  all the day I go about mourning.
For my loins are filled with burning,
  and there is no soundness in my flesh.
I am utterly spent and crushed;
  I groan because of the tumult of my heart.
Lord, all my longing is known to thee,
  my sighing is not hidden from thee.
My heart throbs, my strength fails me;
  and the light of my eyes—it also has gone from me.
My friends and companions stand aloof from my plague,
  and my kinsmen stand afar off.
Those who seek my life lay their snares,
  those who seek my hurt speak of ruin,
  and meditate treachery all the day long.
But I am like a deaf man, I do not hear,
  like a dumb man who does not open his mouth.
Yea, I am like a man who does not hear,
  and in whose mouth are no rebukes.
But for thee, O LORD, do I wait;
  it is thou, O LORD my God, who wilt answer.
For I pray, "Only let them not rejoice over me,
  who boast against me when my foot slips!"
For I am ready to fall, and my pain is ever with me.
  I confess my iniquity, I am sorry for my sin.
Those who are my foes without cause are mighty,
  and many are those who hate me wrongfully.
Those who render me evil for good
  are my adversaries because I follow after good.
Do not forsake me, O LORD!
  O my God, be not far from me!
Make haste to help me,
  O Lord, my salvation! Psalm 38

4 Day 3: **Assessing a Spiritual Need**

1 Read Matthew 9:1-13. (a) Underline what Jesus says (red). (b) Circle each of the people to whom Jesus speaks with a different color. (c) In the margin beside each of Jesus' statements, identify the attitude which characterizes each (such as gentleness, anger, authority and so on).

2 How does Jesus address the paralytic? What is the significance of this form of address?

3 Whose faith caused Jesus to forgive the sick man's sins?

4 What did the faith of the paralytic's friends cause them to do? What does your faith cause you to do for those you know who are in crisis?

5 What do you think the paralytic and his friends were expecting from Jesus? Why do you think Jesus offered him forgiveness?

6 Contrast the response of the scribes with that of the crowd. What do you think accounts for the difference?

7 How was Jesus' calling of Matthew similar to his healing of the paralytic?

8 Compare the Pharisees' response in the last paragraph with the scribes' in the first. What was really the basic concern of both?

9 What does Jesus mean by his closing words in the third paragraph? Who are the well? The sick? The physician? How does Jesus show mercy? What kind of mercy does he demand of us? How could this mercy be demonstrated by you?

And getting into a boat he crossed over and came to his own city. And behold, they brought to him a paralytic, lying on his bed; and when Jesus saw their faith he said to the paralytic, "Take heart, my son; your sins are forgiven." And behold, some of the scribes said to themselves, "This man is blaspheming." But Jesus, knowing their thoughts, said, "Why do you think evil in your hearts? For which is easier, to say, 'Your sins are forgiven,' or to say, 'Rise and walk'? But that you may know that the Son of man has authority on earth to forgive sins"—he then said to the paralytic— "Rise, take up your bed and go home." And he rose and went home. When the crowds saw it, they were afraid, and they glorified God, who had given such authority to men.

As Jesus passed on from there, he saw a man called Matthew sitting at the tax office; and he said to him, "Follow me." And he rose and followed him.

And as he sat at table in the house, behold, many tax collectors and sinners came and sat down with Jesus and his disciples. And when the Pharisees saw this, they said to his disciples, "Why does your teacher eat with tax collectors and sinners?" But when he heard it, he said, "Those who are well have no need of a physician, but those who are sick. Go and learn what this means, 'I desire mercy, and not sacrifice.' For I came not to call the righteous, but sinners." Matthew 9:1-13

4 Day Four: **Caring for the Whole Person**

1 Prior to 1 Kings 19 the prophet Elijah had faithfully served the Lord when most in Israel, including the leaders, were worshiping Baal and Asherah. God had consistently provided for his needs during a time of extreme famine. Just before chapter 19 Elijah had challenged the prophets of Baal to a contest. Each was to pray to their God asking for fire to be sent down from heaven to ignite a sacrifice on an altar. The prophets of Baal were unsuccessful. When Elijah's turn came, he prayed to God who immediately sent down fire that consumed his sacrifice. The people responded by worshiping the Lord and helping Elijah kill the prophets of Baal. (For full details see 1 Kings 17—18.) Suddenly he is confronted by Jezebel. Read 1 Kings 19:1-10, 15-18.

2 Elijah's zeal for the Lord's work had risen to a crescendo just prior to his fearful flight in this passage. Why is it often difficult to hear the Lord's voice when you are feeling especially busy and successful "doing the Lord's work"?

3 What factors probably contributed to Elijah's fear of Jezebel's threat? What had happened to his faith?

4 In two columns, list (a) Elijah's physical, emotional and spiritual needs, and (b) how each need is met:

Needs	Meeting the Needs

5 Consider what you would do in this situation: Your pastor, whom you know well, is being treated for a bleeding ulcer. He is a well-known Christian leader in your area. Many of your friends have become Christians through his ministry. You notice that his personality suddenly changes. No longer bubbly, he often speaks sharply to people with no apparent reason. There is also obvious friction with his family.

Ahab told Jezebel all that Elijah had done, and how he had slain all the prophets with the sword. Then Jezebel sent a messenger to Elijah, saying, "So may the gods do to me, and more also, if I do not make your life as the life of one of them by this time tomorrow." Then he was afraid, and he arose and went for his life, and came to Beer-sheba, which belongs to Judah, and left his servant there.

But he himself went a day's journey into the wilderness, and came and sat down under a broom tree; and he asked that he might die, saying, "It is enough; now, O LORD, take away my life; for I am no better than my fathers." And he lay down and slept under a broom tree; and behold, an angel touched him, and said to him, "Arise and eat." And he looked, and behold, there was at his head a cake baked on hot stones and a jar of water. And he ate and drank, and lay down again. And the angel of the LORD came again a second time, and touched him, and said, "Arise and eat, else the journey will be too great for you." And he arose, and ate and drank, and went in the strength of that food forty days and forty nights to Horeb the mount of God.

And there he came to a cave, and lodged there; and behold, the word of the LORD came to him, and he said to him, "What are you doing here, Elijah?" He said, "I have been very jealous for the LORD, the God of hosts; for the people of Israel have forsaken thy covenant, thrown down thy altars, and slain thy prophets with the sword; and I, even I only, am left; and they seek my life, to take it away." . . .

And the LORD said to him, "Go, return on your way to the wilderness of Damascus; and when you arrive, you shall anoint Hazael to be king over Syria; and Jehu the son of Nimshi you shall anoint to be king over Israel; and Elisha the son of Shaphat of Abel-meholah you shall anoint to be prophet in your place. And him who escapes from the sword of Hazael shall Jehu slay; and him who escapes from the sword of Jehu shall Elisha slay. Yet I will leave seven thousand in Israel, all the knees that have not bowed to Baal, and every mouth that has not kissed him." 1 Kings 19: 1-10, 15-18

4 Day 5: **Thoughts of a Suffering Person**

1 Read Lamentations 3:1-33. Describe the author's concept of God.
2 What is his self-concept?
3 What spiritual needs are expressed in the first seven stanzas?
4 How are these needs met in the last four? For example, what is his source of hope? How does he experience love? How does he experience forgiveness?
5 In what ways are his needs still unmet?
6 If the author were someone you knew, and he expressed only the thoughts in the first seven stanzas, what would you do? Give your rationale.
7 If, after several days, he expressed the thoughts in the last four stanzas, what would you then do? On what basis?

I am one who knows what it is to be punished by God.
He drove me deeper and deeper into darkness
And beat me again and again with merciless blows.

He has left my flesh open and raw, and has broken my bones.
He has shut me in a prison of misery and anguish.

He has forced me to live in the stagnant darkness of death.

He has bound me in chains; I am a prisoner with no hope of escape.
  I cry aloud for help, but God refuses to listen;
  I stagger as I walk; stone walls block me wherever I turn.

He waited for me like a bear; he pounced on me like a lion.
  He chased me off the road, tore me to pieces, and left me.
  He drew his bow and made me the target for his arrows.

He shot his arrows deep into my body.
  People laugh at me all day long; I am a joke to them all.
  Bitter suffering is all he has given me for food and drink.

He rubbed my face in the ground and broke my teeth on rocks.
  I have forgotten what health and peace and happiness are.
  I do not have much longer to live; my hope in the LORD is gone.

The thought of my pain, my homelessness, is bitter poison.
  I think of it constantly,
  and my spirit is depressed.
  Yet hope returns when I remember this one thing:

The LORD's unfailing love and mercy still continue.
  Fresh as the morning, as sure as the sunrise.
  The LORD is all I have, and so in him I put my hope.

The LORD is good to everyone who trusts in him,
  So it is best for us to wait in patience—to wait for him to save us—
  and it is best to learn this patience in our youth.

When we suffer, we should sit alone in silent patience;
  we should bow in submission, for there may still be hope.
  Though beaten and insulted, we should accept it all.

The LORD is merciful and will not reject us forever.
  He may bring us sorrow, but his love for us is sure and strong.
  He takes no pleasure in causing us grief or pain.
Lamentations 3:1-33 (TEV)

4 Day 6 **A Person in Anguish**

1 Read Psalm 22. (a) Underline phrases which indicate a spiritual need and identify each in the margin. (b) Underline physical symptoms in another color.

2 Using the information given in this psalm, summarize the psalmist's: (a) physical status, (b) psychosocial status (self-image, support available, attitude toward illness and so on), and (c) spiritual status (concept of God, source of hope, concept of death and afterlife, use of prayer and so on).

3 Using information from the passage, draw up a care plan:

Needs	Meeting the Needs
Ex: feels God has forsaken him, does not hear him.	Pray with him, express-ing in the prayer those things he feels God has not heard.

4 How could you use this psalm with someone in crisis?

My God, my God, why hast thou forsaken me?
  Why art thou so far from helping me, from the words of my groaning?
O my God, I cry by day, but thou dost not answer;
  and by night, but find no rest.

Yet thou art holy,
  enthroned on the praises of Israel.
In thee our fathers trusted;
  they trusted, and thou didst deliver them.
To thee they cried, and were saved;
  in thee they trusted, and were not disappointed.

But I am a worm, and no man;
  scorned by men, and despised by the people.
All who see me mock at me,
  they make mouths at me, they wag their heads;
"He committed his cause to the LORD; let him deliver him,
  let him rescue him, for he delights in him!"

Yet thou art he who took me from the womb;
  thou didst keep me safe upon my mother's breasts.
Upon thee was I cast from my birth,
  and since my mother bore me thou hast been my God.
Be not far from me,
  for trouble is near
  and there is none to help. . . .

I am poured out like water,
  and all my bones are out of joint;
my heart is like wax,
  it is melted within my breast;
my strength is dried up like a potsherd,
  and my tongue cleaves to my jaws;
  thou dost lay me in the dust of death. . . .

But thou, O LORD, be not far off!
  O thou my help, hasten to my aid! . . .

I will tell of thy name to my brethren;
  in the midst of the congregation I will praise thee:
You who fear the LORD, praise him!
  all you sons of Jacob, glorify him,
  and stand in awe of him, all you sons of Israel!
For he has not despised or abhorred
  the affliction of the afflicted;
and he has not hid his face from him,
  but has heard, when he cried to him.

From thee comes my praise in the great congregation;
  my vows I will pay before those who fear him.
The afflicted shall eat and be satisfied;
  those who seek him shall praise the LORD!
  May your hearts live for ever!
All the ends of the earth shall remember
  and turn to the LORD;
and all the families of the nations
  shall worship before him.
For dominion belongs to the LORD,
  and he rules over the nations.
Psalm 22:1-11, 14-15, 19, 22-28

4 Group Discussion: Meeting Spiritual Needs

1 What are some of the ways that you have found helpful in the past for probing to see if a person has spiritual concerns?

2 Think about the last person you spontaneously prayed with, shared Scripture with or counseled spiritually in response to a need. How did you know that the person had a spiritual need?

3 Share your assessment of the psalmist in Psalm 22 (day six, question 2). How would you attempt to help him (day six, question 3)?

4 Suppose you began talking to a friend over lunch and at one point in the conversation he said, "Since my brother was killed in a car accident last year I haven't been back to church. If God exists, he must be so terrible that I want to stay as far away from him as possible. How could God allow my brother to die? He was only eighteen, had just received a full scholarship to college and was such a great guy." How would you respond at the moment? What plans would you make for follow-up? (Note: Keep in mind the need your friend has to express his feelings as well as the theological statement he has made.)

5 Are you currently involved in a helping relationship? *Without breaking confidences* share some of your concerns with the group so that they can help you assess needs and plan ways to help, and so that you can pray together about your concerns.

5
Resources for Helping People

Anything that directs a person to God,
the ultimate source of health and strength, can
be a means of offering spiritual support
and encouragement in a time of crisis. The four
major resources to be considered this week
include the therapeutic use of yourself,
prayer, the Scriptures and other Christians.

5 Day 1: **Yourself**

1 After reading Romans 12, briefly outline its content.

2 What does the word *sacrifice* mean to you? What does it mean to be a *living sacrifice*?

3 How do we get to know God's will, according to this passage?

4 What should be our attitude about our abilities and talents?

5 The third paragraph describes some of the characteristics of love. List them and write how each might apply in your personal or professional life.

6 The last paragraph gives guidelines for living in harmony with others. List them and write an application for each.

7 Summarize the chapter in a sentence.

I appeal to you therefore, brethren, by the mercies of God, to present your bodies as a living sacrifice, holy and acceptable to God, which is your spiritual worship. Do not be conformed to this world but be transformed by the renewal of your mind, that you may prove what is the will of God, what is good and acceptable and perfect.

For by the grace given to me I bid every one among you not to think of himself more highly than he ought to think, but to think with sober judgment, each according to the measure of faith which God has assigned him. For as in one body we have many members, and all the members do not have the same function, so we, though many, are one body in Christ, and individually members one of another. Having gifts that differ according to the grace given to us, let us use them: if prophecy, in proportion to our faith; if service, in our serving, he who teaches, in his teaching; he who exhorts, in his exhortation; he who contributes, in liberality; he who gives aid, with zeal; he who does acts of mercy, with cheerfulness.

Let love be genuine; hate what is evil, hold fast to what is good; love one another with brotherly affection; outdo one another in showing honor. Never flag in zeal, be aglow with the Spirit, serve the Lord. Rejoice in your hope, be patient in tribulation, be constant in prayer. Contribute to the needs of the saints, practice hospitality.

Bless those who persecute you; bless and do not curse them. Rejoice with those who rejoice, weep with those who weep. Live in harmony with one another; do not be haughty, but associate with the lowly; never be conceited. Repay no one evil for evil, but take thought for what is noble in the sight of all. If possible, so far as it depends upon you, live peaceably with all. Beloved, never avenge yourselves, but leave it to the wrath of God; for it is written, "Vengeance is mine, I will repay, says the Lord." No, "if your enemy is hungry, feed him; if he is thirsty, give him drink; for by so doing you will heap burning coals upon his head." Do not be overcome by evil, but overcome evil with good.
Romans 12

5 Day 2: **Prayer I**

1 In John 14:12-14 what is the key to effective prayer?

2 For what reason does God give us this power in prayer?

3 In Romans 8:26-27 what assistance does Paul say God provides when we don't know how to pray for ourselves? For someone else?

4 How can the Spirit help when you are praying out loud for someone you are with who is in crisis?

5 In 1 Thessalonians 5:16-18 what attitudes are mentioned that should accompany prayer?

6 When should you pray? How can this be done?

7 In James 5:13-18 what specific times for prayer are included?

8 Who does James instruct to pray?

9 What effects does he say prayer can have?

10 How is confession related to prayer?

"Truly, truly, I say to you, he who believes in me will also do the works that I do; and greater works than these will he do, because I go to the Father. Whatever you ask in my name, I will do it, that the Father may be glorified in the Son; if you ask anything in my name, I will do it. John 14: 12-14

Likewise the Spirit helps us in our weakness; for we do not know how to pray as we ought, but the Spirit himself intercedes for us with sighs too deep for words. And he who searches the hearts of men knows what is the mind of the Spirit, because the Spirit intercedes for the saints according to the will of God. Romans 8:26-27

Rejoice always, pray constantly, give thanks in all circumstances; for this is the will of God in Christ Jesus for you. 1 Thessalonians 5:16-18

Is any one among you suffering? Let him pray. Is any cheerful? Let him sing praise. Is any among you sick? Let him call for the elders of the church, and let them pray over him, anointing him with oil in the name of the Lord; and the prayer of faith will save the sick man, and the Lord will raise him up; and if he has committed sins, he will be forgiven. Therefore confess your sins to one another, and pray for one another, that you may be healed. The prayer of a righteous man has great power in its effects. Elijah was a man of like nature with ourselves and he prayed fervently that it might not rain, and for three years and six months it did not rain on the earth. Then he prayed again and the heaven gave rain, and the earth brought forth its fruit. James 5:13-18

5 Day 3: **Prayer II**

1 Read Luke 11:1-13. What causes the disciples to ask Jesus to teach them to pray?

2 What is the significance of Jesus telling the disciples to address God as "Father"?

3 List each petition of Jesus' prayer. Meditate slowly on each phrase. Think about what it would mean to you for God to grant that petition. Write your thoughts.

4 In the first part of the last paragraph, what causes the man to give his friend the bread?

5 What usually causes you to hesitate to ask a friend for help? What is implied about your relationship with a person when you ask him or her for help?

6 How is a Christian's relationship with God like a friendship? In what ways does it surpass friendship?

7 How does your relationship with God compare with your relationship with your parents? Why can God be trusted even more than earthly parents?

8 Read over your personalized version of the Lord's prayer (question 3) and make your meditation a prayer. Trust God to meet your needs and thank him for his faithfulness.

One day Jesus was praying in a certain place. When he had finished, one of his disciples said to him, "Lord, teach us to pray, just as John taught his disciples."

Jesus said to them, "When you pray, say this:
'Father:
May your holy name be honored;
may your Kingdom come.
Give us day by day the food we need.
Forgive us our sins,
for we forgive everyone who does us wrong.
And do not bring us to hard testing.' "

And Jesus said to his disciples, "Suppose one of you should go to a friend's house at midnight and say to him, 'Friend, let me borrow three loaves of bread. A friend of mine who is on a trip has just come to my house, and I don't have any food for him!' And suppose your friend should answer from inside, 'Don't bother me! The door is already locked, and my children and I are in bed. I can't get up and give you anything.' Well, what then? I tell you that even if he will not get up and give you the bread because you are his friend, yet he will get up and give you everything you need because you are not ashamed to keep on asking. And so I say to you: Ask, and you will receive; seek, and you will find; knock, and the door will be opened to you. For everyone who asks will receive, and he who seeks will find, and the door will be opened to anyone who knocks. Would any of you who are fathers give your son a snake when he asks for fish? Or would you give him a scorpion when he asks for an egg? As bad as you are, you know how to give good things to your children. How much more, then, will the Father in heaven give the Holy Spirit to those who ask him!" Luke 11:1-13 (TEV)

5 Day 4: **Scripture: Its Purpose and Power**

1 List in a column the uses of Scripture given in 2 Timothy 3:16-17.

2 Beside each use write down its meaning and/or an example of what it would mean for you.

3 What is the purpose of Scripture given here?

4 How does John 20:30-31 further expand your understanding of the purpose of Scripture?

5 What does Scripture do for us according to Isaiah 55:10-11.

6 What will God's Word accomplish in us?

7 How do 1 Corinthians 15:3-4 and 2 Peter 1:20-21 further expand the purpose and the authority of the Scriptures?

8 Read Psalm 119:9-16 making it your own prayer.

All scripture is inspired by God and profitable for teaching, for reproof, for correction, and for training in righteousness, that the man of God may be complete, equipped for every good work.
2 Timothy 3:16-17

Now Jesus did many other signs in the presence of the disciples, which are not written in this book; but these are written that you may believe that Jesus is the Christ, the Son of God, and that believing you may have life in his name.
John 20:30-31

For as the rain and the snow come down from heaven,
and return not thither but water the earth,
making it bring forth and sprout,
giving seed to the sower and bread to the eater,
so shall my word be that goes forth from my mouth;
it shall not return to me empty,
but it shall accomplish that which I purpose,
and prosper in the thing for which I sent it.
Isaiah 55:10-11

For I delivered to you as of first importance what I also received, that Christ died for our sins in accordance with the scriptures, that he was buried, that he was raised on the third day in accordance with the scriptures.
1 Corinthians 15:3-4

First of all you must understand this, that no prophecy of scripture is a matter of one's own interpretation, because no prophecy ever came by the impulse of man, but men moved by the Holy Spirit spoke from God.
2 Peter 1:20-21

How can a young man keep his way pure?
By guarding it according to thy word.
With my whole heart I seek thee;
let me not wander from thy commandments!
I have laid up thy word in my heart,
that I might not sin against thee.
Blessed be thou, O LORD;
teach me thy statutes!
With my lips I declare
all the ordinances of thy mouth.
In the way of thy testimonies I delight
as much as in all riches.
I will meditate on thy precepts,
and fix my eyes on thy ways.
I will delight in thy statutes;
I will not forget thy word.
Psalm 119:9-16

5 Day 5: **Scripture: Its Impact**

1 Read Psalm 19. What does the creation reveal about God?

2 What have you learned about God through your own observations of nature?

3 If you did not have the Bible and could only learn about God through nature, what would be lacking in your concept of God?

4 The terms *law, commands, worship* and *judgments* in the second stanza are synonyms for Scripture. How does the psalmist describe the Scriptures? How does Scripture affect the psalmist in these verses? How could these effects be beneficial to people in crisis?

5 What is the overall effect of the psalmist's encounter with God through nature and the Scriptures?

6 According to the purposes, power and effects of Scripture you have studied so far, when would it be appropriate to share Scripture with someone in need?

How clearly the sky reveals God's glory!
  How plainly it shows what he has done!
Each day announces it to the following day;
  each night repeats it to the next.
No speech or words are used,
  no sound is heard;
yet their voice goes out to all the world
  and is heard to the ends of the earth.
God made a home in the sky for the sun;
  it comes out in the morning like a happy bridegroom,
  like an athlete eager to run a race.
It starts at one end of the sky and goes across to the other.
  Nothing can hide from its heat.

The law of the LORD is perfect;
  it gives new strength.
The commands of the LORD are trustworthy,
  giving wisdom to those who lack it.
The laws of the LORD are right,
  and those who obey them are happy.
The commands of the LORD are just
  and give understanding to the mind.
The worship of the LORD is good;
  it will continue forever.
The judgments of the LORD are just;
  they are always fair.
They are more desirable than the finest gold;
  they are sweeter than the purest honey.
They give knowledge to me, your servant;
  I am rewarded for obeying them.
No one can see his own errors;
  deliver me, LORD, from hidden faults!
Keep me safe, also, from willful sins;
  don't let them rule over me.
Then I shall be perfect and
  free from the evil of sin.

May my words and my thoughts be acceptable to you,
  O LORD, my refuge and my redeemer! Psalm 19 (TEV)

5 Day 6: **Other Christians**

1 Read 1 Corinthians 12:4-28. (a) Underline the source of spiritual gifts (green). (b) Underline the purpose of the gifts (red). (c) Underline the gifts themselves (blue).

2 Why are different people given different gifts? How is it determined who gets what?

3 Why is it essential for Christians to be in fellowship with other Christians? How are you related to the body of Christ where you live?

4 How does false modesty hinder the work of the church? Prayerfully consider whether you have been refusing to get involved in some form of ministry because you don't feel good enough or brave enough or prepared enough.

5 What effect does an attitude of superiority have on the functioning of the church? In what ways do you feel superior to others in your church or fellowship group? How does your attitude effect your involvement? (For example, a Bible study group of select friends might form to avoid "problem people.")

6 Note the gifts of the Spirit you underlined in blue. Which of these gifts has God given to you? What other gifts has he given you?

7 What responsibilities do we have for each other according to this passage? How can your gifts be used to meet those responsibilities at work, at school and in your community?

8 How has being part of the body of Christ met your personal needs? Do you need to make plans to become more closely related to other Christians?

Now there are varieties of gifts, but the same Spirit; and there are varieties of service, but the same Lord; and there are varieties of working, but it is the same God who inspires them all in every one. To each is given the manifestation of the Spirit for the common good. To one is given through the Spirit the utterance of wisdom, and to another the utterance of knowledge according to the same Spirit, to another faith by the same Spirit, to another gifts of healing by the one Spirit, to another the working of miracles, to another prophecy, to another the ability to distinguish between spirits, to another various kinds of tongues, to another the interpretation of tongues. All these are inspired by one and the same Spirit, who apportions to each one individually as he wills.

For just as the body is one and has many members, and all the members of the body, though many, are one body, so it is with Christ. For by one Spirit we were all baptized into one body—Jews or Greeks, slaves or free—and all were made to drink of one Spirit.

For the body does not consist of one member but of many. If the foot should say, "Because I am not a hand, I do not belong to the body," that would not make it any less a part of the body. And if the ear should say, "Because I am not an eye, I do not belong to the body," that would not make it any less a part of the body. If the whole body were an eye, where would be the hearing? If the whole body were an ear, where would be the sense of smell? But as it is, God arranged the organs in the body, each one of them, as he chose. If all were a single organ, where would the body be? As it is, there are many parts, yet one body. The eye cannot say to the hand, "I have no need of you," nor again the head to the feet, "I have no need of you." On the contrary, the parts of the body which seem to be weaker are indispensable, and those parts of the body which we think less honorable we invest with the greater honor, and our unpresentable parts are treated with greater modesty, which our more presentable parts do not require. But God has so composed the body, giving the greater honor to the inferior part, that there may be no discord in the body, but that the members may have the same care for one another. If one member suffers, all suffer together; if one member is honored, all rejoice together.

Now you are the body of Christ and individually members of it. And God has appointed in the church first apostles, second prophets, third teachers, then workers of miracles, then healers, helpers, administrators, speakers in various kinds of tongues. 1 Corinthians 12:4-28

5 Group Discussion: Resources for Helping People

1 Write down three spiritual gifts you feel God has given you. Now list three spiritual gifts the person on your left seems to have. Go around the circle, sharing the gifts of the person next to you with the group. Ask each person to compare his/her own list. After everyone has shared discuss how you can work together as a group to use the gifts God has given each of you to help people in crisis.

2 How can prayer be used constructively when you are attempting to help others?

3 How did you respond to questions 5-7 of day three (Lk. 11: 1-13)?

4 Share your answers to the questions about Scripture in the day four study.

5 Brainstorm together about which passages of Scripture might be appropriate for people expressing the following thoughts:

(a) "God seems so far away."

(b) "God cares about other people, but he doesn't pay any attention to me."

(c) "Nothing happens when I pray."

(d) "I'm scared! What if I don't graduate?"

(e) "I'm a rotten person. God could never forgive me."

(f) "Life just doesn't seem to make sense anymore."

6 How can you help one another to help others? For example, what kind of support would you like from the others in the group? Share prayer requests and spend some time praying for one another.

6
Personal Resources

It's not just people in crisis
who have spiritual needs. You have them
too. To be able to offer other people as much
help as possible, therefore, your own needs
should be met.

6 Day 1: **Past Experiences**

1 Read 2 Corinthians 1:1-11. Underline what Paul says about God. What is the general tone of this chapter? What do you think Paul is feeling?

2 Last week we read in 1 Corinthians 12, "If one member suffers, all suffer together; if one member is honored, all rejoice together" (v. 26). How does the fourth paragraph give a concrete example of Paul's exhortation?

3 What purpose does Paul see in troubles? Which experiences in your own life have had the effect Paul describes?

4 Note what you underlined about God. How does each of these references reflect God's character and ability to help in times of trouble?

5 You may be struggling with past experiences which still cause you pain. Take a few minutes and talk them over with the Lord. Is there anything you can do to change the situation now? Is there something you need to confess? Are there attitudes you need to change? Commit those memories to the Lord, asking him to help and to heal so that your past hurts would enable you to comfort others.

From Paul, an apostle of Christ Jesus by God's will, and from our brother Timothy—

To the church of God in Corinth, and to all God's people throughout Achaia:

May God our Father and the Lord Jesus Christ give you grace and peace.

Let us give thanks to the God and Father of our Lord Jesus Christ, the merciful Father, the God from whom all help comes! He helps us in all our troubles, so that we are able to help others who have all kinds of troubles, using the same help that we ourselves have received from God. Just as we have a share in Christ's many sufferings, so also through Christ we share in God's great help. If we suffer, it is for your help and salvation; if we are helped, then you too are helped and given the strength to endure with patience the same sufferings that we also endure. So our hope in you is never shaken; we know that just as you share in our sufferings, you also share in the help we receive.

We want to remind you, brothers, of the trouble we had in the province of Asia. The burdens laid upon us were so great and so heavy that we gave up all hope of staying alive. We felt that the death sentence had been passed on us. But this happened so that we should rely, not on ourselves, but only on God, who raises the dead. From such terrible dangers of death he saved us, and will save us; and we have placed our hope in him that he will save us again, as you help us by means of your prayers for us. So it will be that the many prayers for us will be answered, and God will bless us; and many will raise their voices to him in thanksgiving for us.

2 Corinthians 1:1-11 (TEV)

6 Day 2: **A God-given Ministry**

1 Read 2 Corinthians 4. What was Paul's ministry? What principles guide his work? How do these principles apply to your situation?

2 What is his reason for not getting discouraged? How would the content of the last half of the first paragraph protect Paul's sense of purpose even when his work wasn't successful?

3 What are some of the positive effects of troubles that Paul describes? What does trouble teach him about himself? About God?

4 What is Paul's motivation and source of hope in his work?

5 What work has God given you to do? (Be specific and not necessarily limited to your profession.) How do you know God has given you that work?

6 What is your greatest source of discouragement right now? What do you think God may be trying to teach you about yourself through it? What are you learning about God in it? How can Paul's source of motivation and hope be an encouragement to you?

Therefore, having this ministry by the mercy of God, we do not lose heart. We have renounced disgraceful, underhanded ways; we refuse to practice cunning or to tamper with God's word, but by the open statement of the truth we would commend ourselves to every man's conscience in the sight of God. And even if our gospel is veiled, it is veiled only to those who are perishing. In their case the god of this world has blinded the minds of the unbelievers, to keep them from seeing the light of the gospel of the glory of Christ, who is the likeness of God. For what we preach is not ourselves, but Jesus Christ as Lord, with ourselves as your servants for Jesus' sake. For it is the God who said, "Let light shine out of darkness," who has shone in our hearts to give the light of the knowledge of the glory of God in the face of Christ.

But we have this treasure in earthen vessels, to show that the transcendent power belongs to God and not to us. We are afflicted in every way, but not crushed; perplexed, but not driven to despair; persecuted, but not forsaken; struck down, but not destroyed; always carrying in the body the death of Jesus, so that the life of Jesus may also be manifested in our bodies. For while we live we are always being given up to death for Jesus' sake, so that the life of Jesus may be manifested in our mortal flesh. So death is at work in us, but life in you.

Since we have the same spirit of faith as he had who wrote, "I believed, and so I spoke," we too believe, and so we speak, knowing that he who raised the Lord Jesus will raise us also with Jesus and bring us with you into his presence. For it is all for your sake, so that as grace extends to more and more people it may increase thanksgiving, to the glory of God.

So we do not lose heart. Though our outer nature is wasting away, our inner nature is being renewed every day. For this slight momentary affliction is preparing for us an eternal weight of glory beyond all comparison, because we look not to the things that are seen but to the things that are unseen; for the things that are seen are transient, but the things that are unseen are eternal. 2 Corinthians 4

6 Day 3: **God's Spirit in You**

1 Read Romans 8:1-4, 14-18, 22-31. Compare life in the Spirit with life in the flesh (lower nature). What benefits go with the former? Why is suffering still present in the life of Christians?

2 In what ways does God become involved in our lives through the Holy Spirit? How do we experience this?

3 What is the significance of God experiencing human life through Jesus Christ? Why is his suffering important to us?

4 According to this passage what is the meaning of hope? How does it effect our ability to endure suffering?

5 Think of one illness, catastrophe or experience of suffering you fear most. Why does it bother you? Why would it be important to know that even this could not cut you off from God's love?

6 Pull together the evidence Paul gives throughout the chapter that God does care about us. How would you relate this to a person in crisis who begins to question God's concern?

*There is therefore now no condemnation for those who are in Christ
Jesus. For the law of the Spirit of life in Christ Jesus has set me free from
the law of sin and death. For God has done what the law, weakened by
the flesh, could not do: sending his own Son in the likeness of sinful flesh
and for sin, he condemned sin in the flesh, in order that the just re-
quirement of the law might be fulfilled in us, who walk not according to
the flesh but according to the Spirit. . . . For all who are led by the Spirit
of God are sons of God. For you did not receive the spirit of slavery to
fall back into fear, but you have received the spirit of sonship. When we
cry, "Abba! Father!" it is the Spirit himself bearing witness with our spirit
that we are children of God, and if children, then heirs, heirs of God and
fellow heirs with Christ, provided we suffer with him in order that we may
also be glorified with him.*

*I consider that the sufferings of this present time are not worth com-
paring with the glory that is to be revealed to us. . . . We know that the
whole creation has been groaning in travail together until now; and not
only the creation, but we ourselves, who have the first fruits of the Spirit,
groan inwardly as we wait for adoption as sons, the redemption of our
bodies. For in this hope we were saved. Now hope that is seen is not
hope. For who hopes for what he sees? But if we hope for what we do not
see, we wait for it with patience.*

*Likewise the Spirit helps us in our weakness; for we do not know how
to pray as we ought, but the Spirit himself intercedes for us with sighs
too deep for words. And he who searches the hearts of men knows what
is the mind of the Spirit, because the Spirit intercedes for the saints according to the will of God.*

*We know that in everything God works for good with those who love
him, who are called according to his purpose. For those whom he fore-
knew he also predestined to be conformed to the image of his Son, in
order that he might be the first-born among many brethren. And those
whom he predestined he also called; and those whom he called he also
justified; and those whom he justified he also glorified.*

What then shall we say to this? If God is for us, who is against us?
Romans 8:1-4 14-18, 22-31

6 Day 4: **Participants in God's Purpose and Plan**

1 Read Ephesians 1. List the things God has done for us.

2 We live in a time when independence and liberation are primary goals for many people. In contrast, what is the advantage of being "chosen" and "destined"?

3 What does Paul say God's ultimate goal is?

4 What does it mean for you (in practical terms) to live to the praise of God's glory?

5 Paul prays in the last paragraph that the Ephesians would realize certain advantages of their faith in Christ. List these advantages and meditate on each one. How can each aspect of Paul's prayer be realized in your life?

Paul, an apostle of Christ Jesus by the will of God,
  To the saints who are also faithful in Christ Jesus:
  Grace to you and peace from God our Father and the Lord Jesus Christ.

  Blessed be the God and Father of our Lord Jesus Christ, who has blessed us in Christ with every spiritual blessing in the heavenly places, even as he chose us in him before the foundation of the world, that we should be holy and blameless before him. He destined us in love to be his sons through Jesus Christ, according to the purpose of his will, to the praise of his glorious grace which he freely bestowed on us in the Beloved. In him we have redemption through his blood, the forgiveness of our trespasses, according to the riches of his grace which he lavished upon us. For he has made known to us in all wisdom and insight the mystery of his will, according to his purpose which he set forth in Christ as a plan for the fulness of time, to unite all things in him, things in heaven and things on earth.

  In him, according to the purpose of him who accomplishes all things according to the counsel of his will, we who first hoped in Christ have been destined and appointed to live for the praise of his glory. In him you also, who have heard the word of truth, the gospel of your salvation, and have believed in him, were sealed with the promised Holy Spirit, which is the guarantee of our inheritance until we acquire possession of it, to the praise of his glory.

  For this reason, because I have heard of your faith in the Lord Jesus and your love toward all the saints, I do not cease to give thanks for you, remembering you in my prayers, that the God of our Lord Jesus Christ, the Father of glory, may give you a spirit of wisdom and of revelation in the knowledge of him, having the eyes of your hearts enlightened, that you may know what is the hope to which he has called you, what are the riches of his glorious inheritance in the saints, and what is the immeasurable greatness of his power in us who believe, according to the working of his great might which he accomplished in Christ when he raised him from the dead and made him sit at his right hand in the heavenly places, far above all rule and authority and power and dominion, and above every name that is named, not only in this age but also in that which is to come; and he has put all things under his feet and has made him the head over all things for the church, which is his body, the fulness of him who fills all in all. Ephesians 1

6 Day 5: **God's Armor**

1 Read Ephesians 6:10-20. What reason does Paul give for a Christian needing the "whole armor of God"? How does he describe the enemy?

2 What kinds of spiritual opposition do you face?

3 Draw a soldier and put the armor Paul describes on him. Think about each piece of armor. What physical functions does it perform? What is its spiritual counterpart?

4 How can God's armor equip you to face the opposition you listed in question 2? What steps do you need to take to put on the armor?

5 How does prayer make the soldier's equipment complete?

6 Paul concludes by asking the Ephesians to pray for him. If you do not already have people who are committed to praying for you regularly, who could you ask? Who could be your prayer partner? What prayer group might you approach?

Finally, be strong in the Lord and in the strength of his might. Put on the whole armor of God, that you may be able to stand against the wiles of the devil. For we are not contending against flesh and blood, but against the principalities, against the powers, against the world rulers of this present darkness, against the spiritual hosts of wickedness in the heavenly places. Therefore take the whole armor of God, that you may be able to withstand in the evil day, and having done all, to stand. Stand therefore, having girded your loins with truth, and having put on the breastplate of righteousness, and having shod your feet with the equipment of the gospel of peace; besides all these, taking the shield of faith, with which you can quench all the flaming darts of the evil one. And take the helmet of salvation, and the sword of the Spirit, which is the word of God. Pray at all times in the Spirit, with all prayer and supplication. To that end keep alert with all perseverance, making supplication for all the saints, and also for me, that utterance may be given me in opening my mouth boldly to proclaim the mystery of the gospel, for which I am an ambassador in chains; that I may declare it boldly, as I ought to speak.
Ephesians 6:10-20

6 Day 6: **The Lord, Our Shepherd**

Our greatest and most basic resource is the Lord himself. Psalm 23 provides rich imagery of the nature of God's loving care for us. Read through the psalm slowly. Meditate on each phrase asking, What does this mean? and What does it mean *specifically* for me? Write down your thoughts. After you have finished, spend a few minutes thanking God for his goodness to you.

The LORD is my shepherd, I shall not want;
  he makes me lie down in green pastures.
He leads me beside still waters;
  he restores my soul.
He leads me in paths of righteousness
  for his name's sake.

Even though I walk through the valley of the shadow of death,
  I fear no evil;
for thou art with me;
  thy rod and thy staff,
  they comfort me.

Thou preparest a table before me
  in the presence of my enemies;
thou anointest my head with oil,
  my cup overflows.
Surely goodness and mercy shall follow me
  all the days of my life;
and I shall dwell in the house of the LORD
  for ever. Psalm 23

6 Group Discussion: Personal Resources

1 Describe a difficult past experience in your life and share what you learned from it about yourself, other people and God. (Note: If someone shares a current crisis, you may want to stop and pray with that person.)

2 What ministry do you feel that God has given you? How do you know that God has given you that work?

3 What has been the high point of your ministering to people?

4 What has been your greatest source of discouragement?

5 Pray for one another in regard to what has been shared.

6 Think of one illness, catastrophe or experience of suffering that you fear most. What makes it so frightening to you? Why would it be important to know that even this could not cut you off from God's love?

7 Review your list from Ephesians 1 of what God has done for us (day four, question 1). Spend time thanking God for these things.

Appendix A
Nurses Christian Fellowship

Crisis exists on every hand—birth, death, separation, marriage, accident, war, failure. Nurses and nursing students face these and are continually confronted with those who experience them. In crises, people are often more aware of their need for God and for caring people. Nurses Christian Fellowship (NCF) seeks to better prepare nurses and professionals to assist people spiritually, psychosocially and physically as they face crisis. The concern of NCF is for quality nursing care which includes the spiritual dimension and reflects Jesus Christ.

Nurses Christian Fellowship began in Chicago in the mid 1930s with a handful of nurses who shared this concern. In 1948 it was organized nationally with three purposes: (1) to point men and women in nursing who are searching for meaning and purpose in life to Jesus Christ who said, "I am the way, and the truth, and the life"; (2) to urge nurses and students in graduate and undergraduate programs to meet for Bible study, prayer and fellowship that they might become more mature spiritually and increasingly reflect Christlike attitudes and behaviors both personally and professionally; and (3) to declare God's concern for worldwide evangelization and encourage nurses to have a vital role in it.

Toward these ends NCF offers a number of resources. *Persons in Crisis Workshops* are designed for graduates. *Love That Heals Seminars* trains nurses and nonprofessionals. Summer conferences give students and nurses exposure to God's Word and the spiritual dimension of nursing.

Nurses Christian Fellowship also serves over 150 autonomous student groups across the country which espouse NCF's purposes. Together with faculty, nurses and the assistance of more than 25 full-time NCF staff, these groups aim to integrate their faith with their nursing practice.

Literature provided by NCF is another important resource for these individuals and groups. *The Nurses Lamp,* a bimonthly publication, the Missionary Nurse Survey and the Bible study guides mentioned in appendix B are all available through the address below.

Officially Nurses Christian Fellowship is a department of Inter-Varsity Christian Fellowship (IVCF) which is incorporated in the State of Illinois as a nonprofit religious corporation. NCF is represented on IVCF's Board and Corporation by nurses active in the profession. They, together with NCF staff, assist the Director and Area Directors in formulating the program. NCF is represented regularly at the ANA, NLN, NSNA and various state nurses conventions with an exhibit. With no guaranteed income, NCF is dependent on the gifts and prayers of Christian men and women to meet its budget.

Those desiring more information about NCF may write to Nurses Christian Fellowship, 233 Langdon Street, Madison, Wisconsin 53703.

Appendix B
Bible Study Guides

From InterVarsity Press
Rough Edges of the Christian Life. Here are topical studies particularly appropriate for beginning nursing students. Titles include "Who Am I?" "Confidence," "Love," "Fear" and "Anxiety." These studies may be used either in individual or group study. paper, 8 studies
Lifestyle of Love. These studies from John 13—17 focus on Christ and his example for us as nurses. We see him as our role model—helping people in crisis, praying, identifying priorities. paper, 8 studies

From Nurses Christian Fellowship
Lifestyle of Joy. Seven studies from Philippians which focus on saying how we can reflect Jesus Christ in nursing. Studies include "Joy in Serving," "Rejoicing in the Lord," "Christ-Centered Goals" and "Joy in Living and Dying."
Following the Great Physician. Six studies from the Gospels designed to identify principles taught and demonstrated by Jesus Christ for relating with people. Topics include "Offering Peace to People Facing Death," "Communicating Forgiveness" and "Comforting Relatives Experiencing Grief."
Provided We Suffer. One purpose of these studies is to provide a balanced biblical view of suffering and healing. Subjects include "Caring for Those Who Suffer," "Suffering: Used by God" and "Healing: Our Involvement." These studies are best used after *Following the Great Physician.*
Living in Hope. Hope is like love—a feeling, hard to pinpoint, a concept. But more than that, hope is seen in actions which reflect what is inside a person. This series of eight studies includes such topics as "Our Living Hope," "Hope—Where Do You Find It?" "Hope—Based on the Character of God" and "Grieve, But with Hope."
Walking through the Valley. This series of studies helps us look at the scriptural perspective of death and dying. One objective for the studies is to learn to communicate God's love and care to those facing death as well as to their families.
Mental Health: A Biblical Perspective. These eight studies explore mental health as a dynamic mixture of hope, love, joy and peace which guide our relationships with others, and with our past, present and future.

A complete list of study materials with prices is available from Nurses Christian Fellowship, 233 Langdon Street, Madison, WI 53703. Send a stamped, self-addressed envelope with your request for the list.